Walks in
Dumfries & Galloway

Clan Walk Guides

Walks in Dumfries & Galloway

Mary Welsh
and
Christine Isherwood

First Published 2000

ISBN 1 873597 16 9
Text and Illustrations
© Mary Welsh
and
Christine Isherwood

For
Harry Outhwaite

Clan Book Sales Ltd
Clandon House
The Cross, Doune
Perthshire
FK16 6BE

Printed by
Cordfall Ltd, Glasgow

Contents

Contents continued page 6

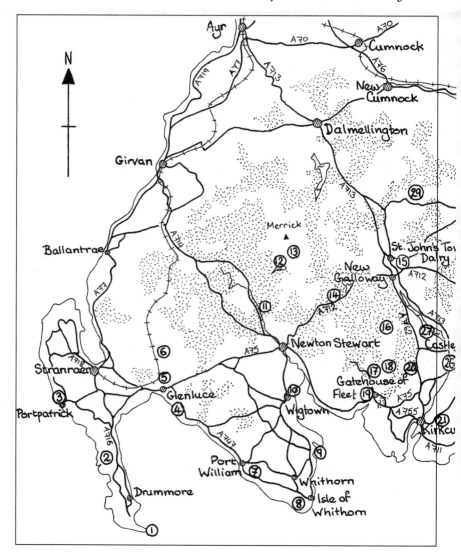

Location Map

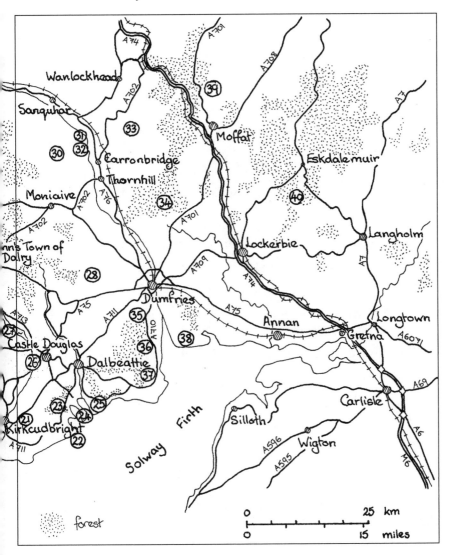

Authors' Note

Please remember on all these walks:

Wear suitable clothes and take adequate waterproofs.

Walk in strong footwear; walking boots are advisable.

Carry the relevant map and know how to use it.

Take extra food and drink as emergency rations.

Carry a whistle; remember six long blasts repeated at one minute intervals is the distress signal.

Do not walk alone, and tell someone where you are going.

If mist descends, return.

Keep all dogs under strict control. Observe all 'No Dogs' notices—they are there for very good reasons.

Readers are advised that while the authors have taken every effort to ensure the accuracy of this guidebook, changes can occur after publication. You should check locally on transport, accommodation, etc. The publisher would welcome notes of any changes. Neither the publisher nor the authors can accept responsibility for errors, omissions or any loss or injury.

1

Mull of Galloway

Park in the Mull of Galloway car park, grid ref. 158305. This lies at the end of the single track road (with passing places) that leads to the lighthouse. To reach the Mull follow the A716 to Drummore and then take the B7041 to its end at a Y-junction. Continue on the left branch along a clearly signposted narrow road.

The Mull of Galloway is Scotland's most southerly point. It is a dramatic windswept headland, almost detached from the remainder of the peninsula. But the wind does not always blow wildly and then the cliff tops, covered in springy turf, are a paradise for walking, from which you have fine views of the teeming bird life. Look for fulmar, kittiwake, razorbill, guillemot, cormorant and shag, which nest on the many ledges of the steep broken cliffs. As you stroll the cliffs, look out to see the Isle of Man, Ireland and the mainland of Scotland.

The walled lighthouse stands beyond the car park. It was built in 1828 by Robert Stevenson to warn ships away from the cliffs and the treacherous tidal currents. It is now automated and the extensive area

Lighthouse, Mull of Galloway

around the buildings is in the care of the Royal Society for the Protection of Birds (RSPB). The Society, in conjunction with several other groups, had plans to open, by April 2000, an interpretative centre in one of the old buildings outside the perimeter wall of the lighthouse itself but within the precinct of the grounds.

Walk 1

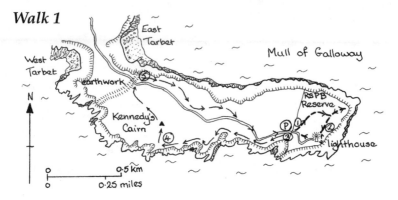

1. Go through the pedestrian gate from the car park into the grounds of the lighthouse. Walk ahead for a few yards and then bear left along a grassy path that passes through large banks of heather. Follow the way as it curves right, passing through two tumbledown walls to join a wide grassy track descending from the lighthouse. Here turn left to walk to the precipitous tip of the Mull and the most southerly point of Scotland. (Please heed the danger sign.)

2. Return along the track and take a narrower path, on the left, to steps leading down to the foghorn. Return by the same path to join the wide grassy track. This joins a reinforced track that takes you to the right of the white and yellow buildings of the lighthouse. Follow the metalled way to the gate into the car park.

3. Cross the car park and walk over the pleasing turf to take a kissing gate in the electrified fence along the southern cliffs. (The fence

Guillemots, razorbills and kittiwakes

8

has been put there to prevent calves falling over the edge. Walkers may walk outside the fence at their own risk or can remain inside and still enjoy magnificent views and sightings of the birds.) Those who go through the kissing gate should turn right and stroll on for half a mile, with care. Continue along the cliff edge until you reach another gate, which you pass through. Those who remain within the fence continue on.

4. Head across the pasture to Kennedy's Cairn. (Local people consulted by the author were uncertain who Kennedy was—some suggested a postman and others a shepherd.) This large stony structure can be climbed by a few rough steps and from the top you can enjoy a scene of rolling inland pastures and the gently curving coastline. Then descend towards the narrow neck of the Mull—barely half a mile wide—to see the 'double dykes' or earthworks. These ditches, stretching from coast to coast, may have been used for defence from about 1000 BC.

5. Cross the road to look down on a small bay on the east coast and then return, climbing steadily along the cliffs. At the fence (put up to keep the cattle off the re-seeded grass) strike right to join the road where there is a gate to allow you to continue upward over the grassy sward. Then return to the road, by a gate, before the steepest ascent. (There was no exit, as this book went to press, through the fence at the top of the sward into the car park.) Here you may wish to return to the car park by the road or by walking up beyond the right side of the wall.

Practicals

Type of walk: A fairly easy walk over rugged cliffs with magnificent views.

Distance: 2 ½ miles/4.2km
Time: 2–3 hours depending on how long you spend
  exploring the earthworks and bird-watching.
Map: OS Landranger 82
Terrain: Generally pathless outside the lighthouse wall; care
  should always be taken on cliffs particularly on a
  windy day.

2

Doon Castle, (Broch), Kirkmadrine Stones, Ardwell Gardens

Car parking details for each of the above are given, below, under the appropriate site. The energetic walker might like to combine walks between two sites, but visiting all three and then returning to the start by foot would be arduous. If two cars are available, however, walkers can conveniently cover in one ramble the 7 miles along delightful narrow lanes from the broch on the west coast to the stone monuments in the centre of the peninsula and then on to the gardens on the east coast.

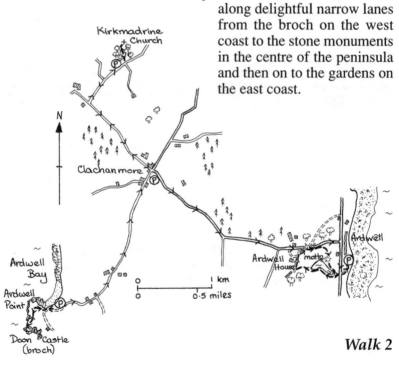

Walk 2

Doon Castle (Broch), Ardwell Point

Parking. There is a large car park, grid ref. 067448, at Ardwell Point. It is approached by a rough, steep, narrow track, with only one passing place. Once you are in the car park, the lovely bay lies immediately in front. Here you can bird-watch and look for common seals, which seem to like observing the activity in the parking area. Alternatively you can leave your car on the verge well before the track, or tuck in tidily at the village of Clachanmore, grid ref. 084467, and walk the two miles to the shore.

Common seal

The walk. From the car park on the shore, continue on the track to a signposted stile directing you to Doon Castle (*circa* 100 BC to AD 200). Beyond the stile, avoid the shallow cliffs to the left and walk the grassy flats and hollows nearer to the craggy shoreline. Go on to the next signposted stile and, once over, follow the path that takes you out along a high rocky promontory, with the sea licking around its base. Here stand the remains of the broch, a circular drystone fortified dwelling. It is now much reduced in height, but must once have dominated the coastline. Originally it had entrances to the seaward and landward sides, the latter protected by a wall and a natural gully. Return the same way, enjoying the thrift, scurvy grass, primrose and sea campion that brighten the sward. Look for gannets, divers, razor bills, cormorants, black guillemots, curlews, oyster catchers and rock pipits as you go. (½ a mile/0.8km)

Kirkmadrine Stones

Parking. To reach the stones, return up the narrow track from the shore, and continue on to the small village of Clachanmore. Turn left and, after less than a mile, take the first right turn. A quarter of a mile along lies the entrance to Kirkmadrine church, grid ref. 080484, where there is very limited roadside parking.

The walk. Turn left through the gates to walk below a fine avenue of trees to the charming church. It is on a hillock, overlooking extensive, pleasing walled pastures. In the 19th century the church was rebuilt from medieval ruins as a burial chapel for Lady McTaggart Stewart of Ardwell. In the glass fronted porch you can see several early Christian monuments. A 5th century stone records in Latin the burial of three priests. Two of the memorials had been used as gateposts and one built into a wall before they were rescued. (¼ mile/0.4km)

Ardwell House Gardens

Parking. To reach these gardens return to Clachanmore and go ahead over the crossroads to Ardwell. Turn right along the A716 to park at the south end of the village in a large car park, on the left, on the shore of Chapel Rossan Bay, grid ref. 110455.

The walk. From the entrance to the car park, cross the A-road and pass through a gap (no signpost) in the low wall of Ardwell House Gardens. Walk ahead along a path through Scots pines to continue beside a stream on your right. Ignore the footbridge and go up the slope. To your right, water overflowing from the lake descends in white cascades stained with peat. Go on to the fence, ignore the stile and turn right, now with the fence to your left. From now on the lovely way takes you beside the lake, known as the Pond. It is fringed with deciduous trees. The vegetation is lush, varied and often exotic and there are well placed seats.

Cross the bridge over the burn at the head of the lake and go on, following the pleasing path. Join an estate road and turn right to pass the charming 17th century Ardwell House, where there is a box for donations. Just beyond, turn right along another estate road and then, before a white painted wooden bridge (which you probably passed under on your journey to Ardwell) turn right again. This takes you along a grassy track through woodland. Go through two metal gates on either side of an estate track and continue through woodland. From here you can glimpse Luce Bay. Leaving the trees, you see a motte (defensive hillock). Cross the footbridge over a dry moat of the motte and climb to the top for another fine view. Continue on the high level grassy path. Then descend gently to leave the Pond to your right. Go on to cross the bridge ignored at the outset of the walk. Turn left to return to the car park on the shore.

3

Portpatrick and Dunskey Glen

As a circular walk this route can be attempted only between Easter and September. Outside this period the glen is closed and the walk will have to be a 'there and back' along the cliff.

Park overlooking the harbour, grid ref. 998541, close to the lifeboat station at Portpatrick. To reach this take the A77 to where it ends on the seafront and then bear right (north).

Portpatrick, in Galloway, and Donaghadee, in Northern Ireland, were the main ferry terminals for crossings of the Irish Sea. In the 1820s Portpatrick's harbour was extended but it was frequently damaged, or closed for days on end, by severe south-westerly gales and finally the trade was transferred to the more sheltered harbour of Stanraer.

Since then Portpatrick has developed as a popular though quiet resort. Picturesque cottages line the harbour overlooked by an impressive Victorian hotel which stands high on the cliffs.

Portpatrick is named after St Patrick, the Christian missionary who, legend would have us believe, crossed the sea from Ireland

Portpatrick harbour

to Scotland in one great stride. In the heart of the village are the ruins of the 17th century parish church, which has a round tower. Here many runaway marriages were performed.

The walk begins at the same place as the Southern Upland Way (SUW) begins its 212 mile, coast to coast, long distance footpath to Cocksburnpath on the eastern seaboard.

Walk 3

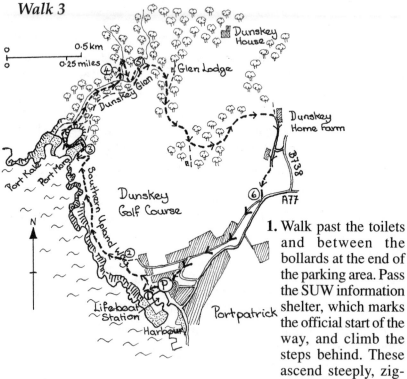

1. Walk past the toilets and between the bollards at the end of the parking area. Pass the SUW information shelter, which marks the official start of the way, and climb the steps behind. These ascend steeply, zig-zagging to ease the gradient, and bring you to the cliff top. Follow the well marked route as it winds left and continues along a lane to the left of a golf course. The lane soon becomes a track and then a narrow path along the cliff top.

2. Walk the delightful way, high up but safely away from the edge, with magnificent views out to sea and of the waves crashing on the jagged rocks below. The path leads to rough stony steps that zig-zag down to Port Mora, a tiny sandy bay, with a pebbly shore. At the foot of the steps a fine waterfall descends and the burn then cuts its way through the sand to the sea.

14

3. Cross the beach to take a grassy track going inland. After a few yards take the signposted steps on the left and follow a path to Port Kale, another quiet sandy beach, where the breakers come rolling in. Here leave the SUW and follow a wide track inland, passing a white wooden building on your right. Go on ahead with the Dunskey Burn to your left. Walk the delightful track, with the steep tree-clad sides of the Dunksey Glen rearing upwards to your left and right.

4. The path brings you to a footbridge across the burn, with the head of the glen rising steeply in front of you. Cross the bridge and walk steadily uphill through pleasing woodland, with a tributary of the burn beside you. Follow the path as it winds right to cross the tributary and then climb again so that you can look down to the path you have just walked. At a Y-junction of needle-strewn tracks, the right branch leads to a viewpoint into the glen and the other continues to a fine bridge over the main burn at a point where it descends in tempestuous cascades.

5. Cross the bridge and go on ahead along a narrow reinforced path to join a forest road, where you turn left. Stroll on along this to a T-junction of tracks, where you walk right. Remain on this track to reach the home farm, where you bear right. At the next Y-junction take the right branch to carry on along a small stretch of metalled road in front of several houses. Beyond, a pleasing track descends, beside woodland on the left, to join the A77. Turn right.

6. After half a dozen steps bear right into a secondary road to walk above the A-road and parallel with it. Take the first left, Braestead Road, to begin your descent towards the harbour. Watch out for the flight steps, on the right, that go on down and bring you, after a short stretch along the continuing road, to the car park.

Practicals

Type of walk: A lovely walk along fine cliffs followed by a delightful stroll through a glen set in deciduous woodland.

Distance:	3 ½ miles/5.6km
Time:	2 hours
Map:	OS Landranger 82
Terrain:	Some steepish climbs but generally easy walking all the way.

4

Glenluce, Auchenmalg, Stairhaven

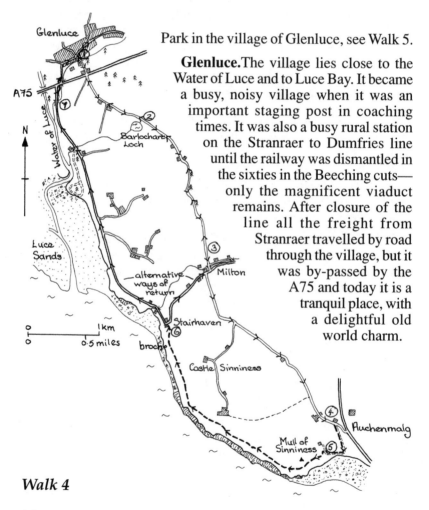

Park in the village of Glenluce, see Walk 5.

Glenluce. The village lies close to the Water of Luce and to Luce Bay. It became a busy, noisy village when it was an important staging post in coaching times. It was also a busy rural station on the Stranraer to Dumfries line until the railway was dismantled in the sixties in the Beeching cuts— only the magnificent viaduct remains. After closure of the line all the freight from Stranraer travelled by road through the village, but it was by-passed by the A75 and today it is a tranquil place, with a delightful old world charm.

Walk 4

The broch-like structure, called 'broken castle' locally, is situated on a rocky eminence, 100ft above the east shore of Luce Bay. It is bounded and overshadowed on the landward side by a steep coastal slope beneath which is a deep gully. This is a strong natural defensive position but there is still an element of doubt about whether it was a broch. A hundred years ago its stones were disturbed when a whisky still was built among the boulders.

1. With your back to the Public Hall in the centre of Glenluce walk left. Turn left into Bankfield road. Cross the bridge over Lady Burn and continue up the quiet pretty lane. With great care go over the very busy A75 and continue up the narrow lane ahead. As you go look right for a fine view of Luce Bay.

2. Go on along the metalled way to pass, away to your right, Barlochart Loch, which is surrounded by reeds and shrubby trees. Soon the lane has grass along the middle and it climbs and dips gently as it passes through a rolling patchwork of walled fields, with wide and long extensive views. Follow the lane as it bears right, where in winter fieldfare and redwing flock and the hedgerows are bright with snowdrops.

3. Cross Milton Burn and continue to Milton. Here turn right and then immediately left to go on along another very narrow lane. Look right to see the ruins of Castle Sinniness. Beside the road you might disturb a sparrowhawk or spot reed buntings feeding among tussocks of grass. Head on until the road appears to dip into the sea. Once over the brow the way drops down to pass Long Forth farm. To your left, as you approach Auchenmalg, you can view, over green pastures, headland after headland, stretching away into the misty distance.

4. Go on down into a lush hollow and, just before a house on the right and opposite a second on the left, take the track going off right, signposted The Barracks. Walk the pleasing way, where the bushes about the track are the haunt of spring migrants. And then the track swings right to pass above the sandy and pebbly shore of Auchenmalg Bay. Ahead lies the Mull of Sinniness—the way the walk continues. Go on where the track becomes tarmacked and bears inland. Cross, on the left, the signposted small wooden footbridge over a ditch.

5. Beyond climb the steps that take you up the steeply rising way

through the gorse to the clifftop. Turn left and follow the waymarked route, with the sea to your left. This lovely coastal way was opened at Easter 2000. It goes on for nearly three miles, is well stiled and waymarked, and is a delight to walk. After two miles look down the inaccessible steep cliffs to the remains of a broch just above the shore. (Do not attempt to visit it by climbing down the cliffs or walking along the shore.) Follow the path as it descends steeply to a stile to Stairhaven.

6. At the narrow road you have a choice. You can either walk left along the coast road to return to Glenluce (see below) or turn right to walk to Milton and then go left to rewalk your outward route. To walk along the coast road, continue left over the sturdy newly reinforced bridge over the Milton Burn. On the sands to your left are toilets and picnic tables. Take care as you go because, depending on the season, the road can be busy. It has no pavement and only intermittent grass verges but the views are superb, ranging over the vast expanse of Luce Bay and beyond to the Mull of Galloway. Listen and look for curlews, oyster catchers, pintails, common gulls and redshanks.

7. Gradually the road becomes wider and moves inland to pass beside great banks of gorse. It comes close to the Water of Luce and then the Lady Burn. Don't miss, on the right, the entrance to the underpass that takes you under the A75. Walk on and then bear right to return to Glenluce.

Practicals

Type of walk: A pleasing walk of contrasts.

Distance:	9 miles/14.5km
Time:	5 hours
Map:	OS Landranger 82
Terrain:	The lanes to Auchenmalg are a delight to walk and you will rarely encounter a vehicle. The coastal path is steep at the beginning and at the end. It is generally easy going but if, in the winter, the cows have trampled an area around their feeding station on the cliffs, it becomes a challenge to continue on the path. Route suitable for fit walkers. Walking boots essential.

Glenluce Abbey

Park in the signposted car park in the centre of Glenluce village. It lies to the north side of Main Street, grid ref. 198577.

The Abbey. The picturesque ruins of Glenluce Abbey can be reached by a 2 ½ mile return walk (1 ¼ miles each way) over fields, following the line of an ancient track between the abbey and the village. The abbey was founded by Roland, Lord of Galloway, in 1190. Several communities of monks lived here, creating gardens and productive orchards. The monks embraced poverty as a way of life. Important visitors included King Robert I, James IV and Mary Queen of Scots on their pilgrimages to Whithorn. The abbey was destroyed during the Reformation. It is open daily throughout the summer and weekends during the winter.

1. From the Public Hall, housing the tourist information centre and toilets, cross the road and walk up the steeply rising Church Street. Cross the railway bridge and go on along the very narrow lane until you reach a T-junction. Ignore the left turn and cross the road to

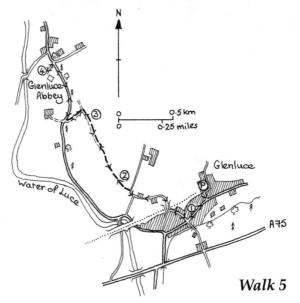

Walk 5

climb a fine ladderstile that you can see ahead. Beyond continue beside the boundary on your right.

2. Cross the next stile and remain by the hedge on your right. Drop down to a stile over a small stream. Once over, carry on, keeping the wall to your left. The next stile gives access to a track.

3. Continue ahead. Then take a concreted track going off left and follow it downhill to reach the road from Glenluce to New Luce. Turn right and walk with care to the abbey, the ruins of which you can see across the field.

4. To return retrace your outward route, enjoying spectacular views of Luce Bay.

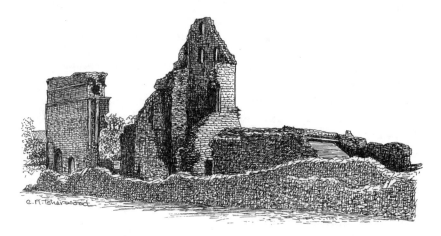

Glenluce Abbey

Practicals

Type of walk: A delightful waymarked short walk to a picturesque ruin.

Distance:	2 ½ miles/4km
Time:	One hour's walking
Map:	OS Landranger 82
Terrain:	Easy walking. Expect plenty of mud in the winter.

New Luce, Cruise, Kilhern, Caves of Kilhern, Loups of Barnshangan

Park in New Luce Village Hall car park, grid ref. 175649. To reach New Luce leave the A75 at Glen Luce and take the B-road, north, signposted New Luce.

New Luce. An attractive village, with many of its old cottages restored. It stands at the junction of the Main Water of Luce and the Cross Water of Luce. Five minor roads meet at the village, but there is little traffic. This walk makes use of two of these roads and starts at the Southern Upland Way (SUW) information shelter at the north end of Main Street.

Caves of Kilhern. This is a Neolithic chambered long cairn, a communal burial place, constructed some 4000 to 5000 years ago.

Caves of Kilhern

The remains of four stone-lined chambers can be seen within the cairn. The eastern chamber is the most complete, retaining its cap stone. Nothing remains of the contents of the burial chambers, these having been desecrated in the past.

Loups of Barnshangan. Falls on the Cross Water of Luce. These can just be seen from the minor road if the vegetation is not too high. A rickety stile leads to a long, unsteady, wooden footbridge from where the delightful white cascades, flecked with the bronze stain of peat, can be viewed.

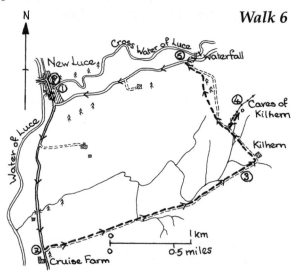

Walk 6

1. Start from the SUW shelter to walk through the pleasing village. Stride the bridge over the Cross Water of Luce and go on to pass, on your left, the church. Continue on, using the grass verges where possible, along the quiet road for 1 ½ miles.

2. At Cruise farm, which lies to your right, look for the ladderstile opposite, the start of a moorland section of the SUW. Climb the stile and continue up the track beyond. The wide clear straight way, well waymarked, continues ahead for 1 ¾ miles of wild moorland, with extensive views on either side. In summer the air is filled with the calls of curlews, meadow pipits and skylarks. In winter it is a quiet, lonely place where your only company will be the shaggy Galloway cattle and a few frogs in the pools along the very, very muddy track.

3. Watch for your first glimpse of the ruined farm of Kilhern. As you approach, the track becomes grassy and a delight to tread. By the farm's boundary wall a SUW waymarker directs you left, along the continuing track. Remain on this as it traverses the moorland until you can see a tall ladderstile over a wall ahead. This is the point to walk, right, across the heather moorland to visit the Long Cairn, which stands on a hillock close to the wall. Wander around the site to see the cairns, one of which still has its cap stone.

4. Return to the track and climb the ladderstile. Press on along the track, gradually leaving the moorland behind. Go under a wire fence that goes across the SUW and continue gently downwards beside the wall on your right, over waymarked grassy slopes. Go past a conifer plantation on the right. Enjoy the pleasing view of the Cross Water of Luce, winding through the valley bottom, and then follow a track down to a minor road.

5. To see the small waterfall, walk right and look for the stile in the wall, now on your left. A few steps further on you might see it over the wall. Return to where you joined the road and carry on, gently downhill, along the quiet way to New Luce. At the church, passed just as you left the village, turn right to return to the start of the walk.

Practicals

Type of walk: Half of this walk is along quiet roads and the other half over rolling lonely heather moorland along the Southern Upland Way. A visit to the Caves of Kilhern is a great bonus.

Distance:	6 miles/9.6km
Time:	3 hours
Map:	OS Landranger 82
Terrain:	The moorland tracks can be muddy after rain and very muddy in the winter.

7

Kirkmaiden Church, Gavin Maxwell Memorial, Monreith House, Drumtroddan Stones

Park in the shore car park at Back Bay, near Monreith, grid ref. 365395. To reach this turn off the A747, south-east of Monreith, into a narrow lane, heading towards the sea and clearly signposted 'Gavin Maxwell Memorial'. The parking area lies at the very end of the narrow road.

Kirkmaiden. The picturesque church of St Medana or Kirkmaiden lies tucked up against the cliff face. It dates from the 12th century and is partly ruinous. In the kirkyard some of the tombstones date from the 16th and 17th century and there are remnants of ancient crosses. The intact part of the church (generally locked) has Victorian renovations and is used as a mausoleum for the Maxwell family.

Gavin Maxwell Memorial. Sitting atop a rocky outcrop on a grassy hillock, close to the narrow road to the shore, is a bronze otter, commemorating the life and writings of Gavin Maxwell. From the hillock, enjoy what was believed to have been one of his favourite views along the delightful coastline. A nearby plaque says, 'This place he loved as a boy and made famous as a man.'

Monreith House. Delightful tracks and paths take you on a circular walk through the grounds of Monreith House and its White Loch of Myrton. From one of these tracks you have an excellent view of the house, the former home of Gavin Maxwell.

NB Some of the walks around Monreith House are sometimes

24

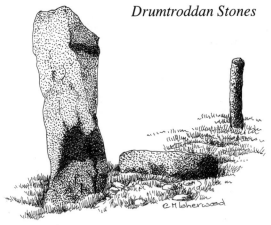

Drumtroddan Stones

closed for shooting parties between October and January.

Drumtroddan Stones. Two erect stones and one fallen one can be seen from the road. They are believed to date from about 2000 to 1500 BC. The reason for placing the stones here and for what purpose is not known.

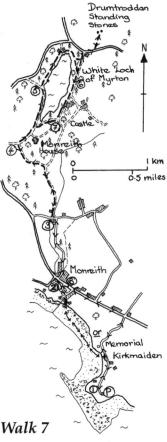

1. From the car park, walk back along the narrow road, with fine views of the shore and the high craggy cliffs, pink with thrift in early summer. When opposite the white fencing of the golf club, take a grassy trod, left, to visit Kirkmaiden church. From just before the wall of the kirkyard steps lead down to the shore. If the tide is out, descend these and walk right, west, along the sandy and pebbly beach. Go round the headland and stroll on to take, just before a stream rushing out to sea, a track leading inland to the village of Monreith. If the tide is high or coming in, return from Kirkmaiden to the narrow road and continue uphill, visiting the otter memorial as you go. Continue to the A747. Turn left and walk, with care, into the village.

2. If coming from the shore turn left. Using either route continue, with the terrace of cottages to your right. These were built to house workers

Walk 7

at the long-disused brickworks. Just before the A-road makes a sharp left turn and the B7085 continues to Wigtown, take a minor road, on the right, that leads into a small housing estate. Keep to the left of a small white church-like building, the village hall, and continue along a pleasing hedged green lane.

3. At a T-junction of tracks, turn left, cross the burn and then, almost immediately, right. Stride on to pass, on the left, Bridge Lodge. After passing through three gates, bear half left, following a tractor route across the pasture. Look left to see an amazing elongated copse of sixty or more monkey-puzzle trees. Go through the next gate into fine woodland and continue to a T-junction. Turn left to walk along the edge of the mixed woodland. The track winds right, still on the edge of the trees.

4. At a metalled estate road, turn right to walk along the pleasing way, with Monreith House beyond the trees to your right. Ignore the track to the house and go on along the continuing way, soon to come close to the tranquil White Loch of Myrton. In spring, autumn and winter look for teal, cormorants and goldeneye. Enjoy the reed fringed loch, with otter spraints on the rocks beside the water. Pass the fishing area, where anglers hope for bites from perch, rudd and pike.

5. Leave the track to take a narrower waymarked path which keeps near to the loch. Go past a cottage and bear right, following the lochshore. At a Y-junction take the left branch to climb up through the trees to join an estate road. Turn left at the Lodge, then right onto the B7021 and walk for 100 yards to a gate on the left. Go through and walk across the pasture to another gate to see the stones and read

Snowdrops

26

the explanatory plaque. Return to the road and retrace your steps, by turning right and then taking the next left at the Lodge.

6. Ignore your exit track from the loch and walk on. Then take a track on the right in the direction of the Dourie farm office. Stroll on past the ruin of the 15th century Myrton Castle, almost hidden from view by the trees. Only the tower survives. This was built by the McCulloch, master falconers to the crown of Scotland.

7. Two hundred and fifty yards along and just before a 'Private' sign beside the track leading to Monreith House, turn right. From this track you have a fine view of Monreith House. Continue on to retrace your outward route. After passing the access road to the house, remember to take the next left turn to walk round the edge of the woodland. Don't miss the right turn to the gate below the monkey-puzzle trees. Follow the tractor track across the pasture and go on through three gates. At the T-junction, turn left, cross the burn and then, beyond Burnside Cottage, walk right to return to Monreith.

8. Turn left and, if the tide is out, cross the road to take the track leading to the shore, and walk left to return to the car park. If the tide is too high, walk along the A-road, with care, to take the signposted right turn and follow the minor road to the car park. If you failed to visit the Gavin Maxwell Memorial at the start of your walk, you will have another chance to do so on your right as you go.

Practicals

Type of walk: An enjoyable walk starting from a pretty bay and visiting a ruined church and a sculpture. It continues through gentle countryside to a fine house with pleasing gardens and a loch fringed with deciduous woodland.

Distance: 7 ½ miles/12km
Time: 3–4 hours
Map: OS Landranger 83
Terrain: Easy walking all the way.

8

Isle of Whithorn to St Ninian's Cave

Park in the well signposted parking area, grid ref. 477363, beside the mud and shingle foreshore of the village of the Isle of Whithorn, which should not be confused with the larger village of Whithorn. To reach the Isle of Whithorn leave the A746 at Whithorn and take the B7004 for 6 miles to the shore. Here the road bears slightly left, with the sea to your right. The parking area and toilets are on the left.

Isle of Whithorn. From the parking area the road continues on past the fine church on the shore and then winds round to cross a causeway onto the island. Before the causeway was built the shingle bar that connected the island and the mainland, creating a safe harbour, was covered by the sea at high tide. Now picturesque cottages and houses line one side of the road. The tide licks their back gardens and, on the other side of the road, comes almost to the doorstep of the red corrugated yacht club. Irish pilgrims landed at the Isle of Whithorn on their way to visit St Ninian's shrine at Whithorn Priory. To the east of the harbour lies the ruined St Ninian's chapel, which dates from early in the 12th century. Further on, on the highest point on the isle, is a fine white tower once used for signalling the state of the tides to approaching sailing ships.

Whithorn. A linear village, its narrow streets lined with 18th and 19th century cottages. Here Ninian, a Roman trained Briton, arrived around AD 400, with a directive from Rome to spread Christianity throughout Scotland. The first Christian centre he established was known as the White House (from this comes the name of the village). Several centuries later a great monastery was built and Whithorn became a centre of pilgrimage. Since the middle of the 1980s archeologists have been excavating the monastery ruins, 'The Whithorn Dig'. Visit the local museum, close-by, to see the many artefacts recovered.

St Ninian's Cave. This is to be found on the coast, west of the villages of Whithorn and the Isle of Whithorn. According to legend, St Ninian often retreated to the cave for contemplation. Since his time many pilgrims have visited the cave.

View from St Ninian's Cave, Whithorn

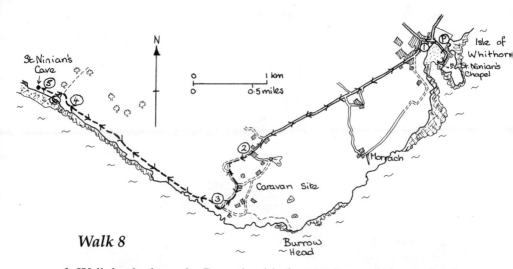

Walk 8

1. Walk back along the B-road, with the sea to your left, to take the first left for Burrow Head. This minor road soon takes you out into rolling countryside, where vast acres of gorse flower for many months of the year, the bushes the haunt of stonechats. Continue ahead for nearly two miles, ignoring all tracks and roads going off left and right.

2. Pass through two fine gateposts and go on. Follow the road as it winds left. As you near a caravan site, bear left towards the reception building and then, just before it, go right, heading for the shore.

3. Near the cliff edge bear right to walk along a grand path over springy turf. This leads to a gate and a signpost for the coastal way. Pause here to look out towards the Isle of Man. Stride on along the clear path, to step across three small streams, which hurry towards the sea. As you go watch for herring gulls, lesser black-backed gulls, fulmars and cormorants either circling over the sea or 'sunbathing' on the jagged-topped rocks just off-shore. Continue on where the path moves outside the cliff fence. At times the way is narrow and the cliff face sheer. Care should be taken and children kept under close control.

Fulmar

30

4. After a mile and a half of magnificent cliff walking, you reach another signposted gate. Beyond, keep to the path nearest the sea to descend the cliff to join the pebble beach of Port Castle Bay. Ahead, in the far cliff face, you can see St Ninian's cave. Aim for it, finding the easiest way over the rounded boulders. Keep to the shore side to avoid crossing the burn issuing out of Physgill Glen. Very rarely, the tide might be so high it prevents you from crossing the beach to the cave.

5. A small ramp of boulders and shingle brings you to a rock platform in front of the shallow cave. St Ninian chose well, as the 'stranded' craggy boulders in front of the cave must have sheltered him from most winds off the sea. He would have enjoyed the pair of buzzards that today ride the thermals above and the kestrels quartering the path that goes inland beside the burn.

6. Return across the beach and climb the signposted cliff to return along the pleasing cliff path. Then head inland, keeping the caravan site to your right. Follow the road as it winds left back to Isle of Whithorn.

NB **Do not be tempted to follow the path on the map that continues along the cliffs to Burrow Head and then on to the farm named Morrach. This path very quickly moves out onto the sea side of the wire fence, becoming very narrow and being positioned right at the edge of sheer drops. Sometimes there is no way through the gorse and no access back through the fence.**

Practicals

Type of walk: After walking a quiet narrow lane the way continues along magnificent cliffs, with superb views, to reach the cave above the shore.

Distance:	9 miles/14.4km
Time:	4–5 hours
Map:	OS Landranger 83
Terrain:	Easy walking all the way but take care along a short distance of the coastal path which comes close to the cliff edge.

9

Garlieston, Rigg Bay, Cruggleton Castle, Galloway House

Park in the public car park on the shore road at the south end of Garlieston, grid ref. 479463. To reach the village, leave the A746 at Sorbie, heading east along the B7052.

Garlieston. Lord Garlies, heir to the Earl of Galloway, designed the village of Garlieston in 1760. It was built on the edge of his large wooded estate. Two rows of two-storey colour-washed houses follow the curve of the bay. The village is protected by a sea wall against high tides. Ship building developed during the 19th century. Rope and sailcloth was made in the village mill. The pier was built in about 1816 when local produce was exported abroad and goods including tea and lace, lime and coal were brought into Garlieston to be distributed throughout southern Scotland. The village is now a conservation area.

Cruggleton Castle from Sliddery Point

Galloway House gardens were created in 1740 by Lord Garlies. The house stands ⅝ mile from the village and the pleasing woodlands stretch down to sandy Rigg Bay. The 'woodland walk' and 'shore walk', both a delight, are open to the public. Just offshore look for curlews, greenshanks, redshanks, shelduck, ringed plover, knot, dunlin, oyster catchers, mergansers, dabchick and herons. Watch for snipe in the wet flushes beside the paths. (The grounds are managed by a charitable trust and admission charges are collected in an honesty box at the car park for Galloway House. The house itself is not open to the public.)

Cruggleton Castle. The 13th century castle was once the main home of the Lords of Galloway. The castle has been inhabited periodically since the first century. Previously thought to be impregnable, it was captured by Robert Bruce on his mission to free Scotland from English rule in 1308. All that remains today is a solitary archway and several intriguing walled hollows. It stands high on the cliffs, with sheer drops on two sides. There are tremendous views up and down the magnificent coast. Visitors should approach with care as there is nothing to protect them from the sudden drop to the shore far below.

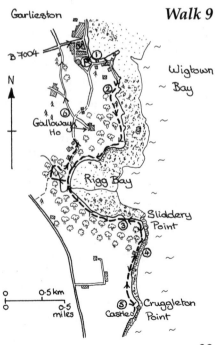

Walk 9

1. Walk east from the car park to pass, on your left, the toilets, the village hall and a memorial to the building and testing, at Garlieston in 1943, of the 'Mulberry harbour', for use in Normandy during the 1939–45 war. Walk on to pass the austere old rope and sail factory. Go on to take a pleasing track along the shore, with the sea to your left. Beyond a gate, the way continues, almost pathless, but easy underfoot.

2. Pass through an iris bed and a mass of rhododendrons,

Greenshanks

the haunt of small song birds. Then you can see stately Galloway House to the right. Continue on the path, with trees on both sides and the sea sparkling away to the left. Here you might spot roe deer. At the Y-junction, follow the arrowed directions for the 'shore path' to continue your walk round the sand and shingle of Rigg Bay. Out to sea you can see part of the Mulberry harbour. Watch for the waymark directing your right, and then immediately left, to continue on through woodland to a low signpost. Take the direction (left) for Cruggleton Castle.

3. The waymarked path continues through trees, crosses several footbridges over hurrying streams and then begins to climb gently (look for yellow painted bands on trees if in doubt over the route). Go on ascending up to Sliddery Point, where an arrow directs you to a seat. Here you realise how high you have climbed and can enjoy a dramatic view of the sheer-sided cliffs and a first glimpse of the ruined castle.

4. Stroll on through the trees to come to a ruined cottage. Go through the iron gate beside it, with a notice warning you of dangerous cliffs. The path continues out onto the open cliffs, but keeps safely close to the wall on your right. Stroll on to climb a ladderstile over the wall and walk on. Beyond the next ladderstile a signpost directs to yet another into the precincts of the ruins. From here there are tremendous views along the coast and across Wigtown Bay.

5. Return back by the same route to Rigg Bay. Once into the trees, go on a short distance to the low signpost for the 'woodland walk' (at the point where you followed the other arm of the signboard for Cruggleton Castle). Walk the good track left and then right and continue where it winds right. Cross several footbridges to reach another track, where you turn left. Once the way becomes tarmacked, follow it as it winds left to pass through the car park with the honesty box.

Rock dove

6. Press on along the quiet access road. As you near the B-road, cut across the corner, right, to go on along a wide green verge edging the road. Continue until you reach the Queen's Arms Hotel. Turn right to walk down High Street, and then left to reach the car park.

Practicals

Type of walk: A very pleasant walk along the shore. Then the way continues uphill through deciduous woodland and on along cliffs to a ruined castle.

Distance: 6 ½ miles/10.5km
Time: 3–4 hours
Map: OS Landranger 83
Terrain: Easy walking all the way.

10

Wigtown

Park in the large open area in the centre of Wigtown's main street, grid ref. 434555. The town is reached by the A714 from Newton Stewart.

Wigtown was once the medieval capital of the region, and was made a royal burgh in 1292. It had a castle of which there is now little trace. Today it is Scotland's book town, with 18 book-related businesses clustering around the town centre, a huge elongated open area along its main street. It has two market crosses and the square is lined in parts with pastel-coloured houses The views from several of its footpaths are superb—across the salt flats and Wigtown Bay to the Galloway Hills beyond.

The Wigtown Martyrs. The Covenanter movement refused to accept Charles II as head of the Scottish church. In 1638 the Scots had set up the Covenant of Protest, from which the word Covenanter derives, challenging the power of Charles to appoint church ministers. Non-conforming ministers held services outdoors and those attending could be put to death. Margaret Wilson and Margaret McLaughlin, of Wigtown, were in sympathy

Martyr's Stake, Wigtown

with the movement In 1685 they were tied to a stake in the estuary of the River Bladnoch and left to drown as the tide came in. This walk visits the site, but today rarely is there a tide to be seen as a huge saltmarsh and mudflats have built up. The memorial is reached by duckboards stretching out into the marsh.

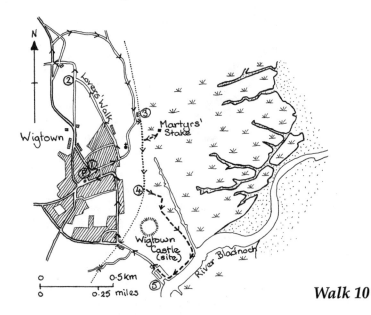

Walk 10

1. From where you have parked head towards the County Buildings, a huge Victorian French Gothic town hall, which you cannot miss. To its left is Moss Road; follow it downhill towards the church. Turn left before the church and walk Church Lane to come to a signpost directing you ahead along Lovers' Walk. Enjoy the magnificent views across the bay to the hills as you climb the hedged way. Here in spring look for large cushions of white violets and for pink footed geese, in vast numbers, feeding on the saltmarsh below.

2. At the T-junction of tracks, turn right and go on the gated way to the A714, where you turn right. With care, walk for 200 yds along the wide verge to take, on the right again, a minor road in the direction of the Moss of Cree. From here Cairnsmore of Fleet dominates the bay from the other side. At the T-junction, turn right and walk on along the delightful way, following the signs for the

Bullfinch

Martyrs' Stake. At the corner, turn left, directed by another sign for the stake. Before you go on, turn left again, to pause in the bird hide of the Wigtown Bay local nature reserve, from where you can observe the mudflats and salt marsh. In summer this is a breeding area for common sandpiper, common and black-headed gull, lapwing and curlew. From October until late April it supports innumerable pink footed geese. From the hide you can look across the bay to Creetown.

3. Leave the hide and continue on along the old Wigtown railway line, where the last train ran in 1964. This was also the site of Wigtown Harbour until 1817 when the River Bladnoch, which flows into the bay, changed its course. Turn left to walk the duckboards over the saltmarsh to the monument erected on the supposed site where the two Margarets died. From this sombre spot, with its incredible view, return to the old railway track and walk on. Continue past a small picnic area on the left and on through a gate. The grassy way is hedged on both sides and the bushes and trees are full of songbirds, making it a joy to walk.

White violets

4. Just before the metalled gate across the track, look for the embankment stretching away left and descend to a stile to walk the fenced way, with marshland on either side. Again enjoy the magnificent views as you walk the breezy way. Follow the embanked path as it curves right and comes beside the River Bladnoch. Continue on until you come to a stile and steps into a small car park beside the present harbour. This was built in 1817 to replace the earlier one and once it was much used by freight and fishing boats. But now only leisure craft are seen. This is a good area for a picnic.

Male reed bunting

5. Turn right and walk along a track. In the field to your right is the site of Wigtown Castle—perhaps the few stones in the pasture were part of it. Cross the bridge over the disused railway track and turn right to walk Harbour Road and then left along South Main Street to arrive close to the town hall.

Practicals

Type of walk: An exhilarating walk through the countryside and along the shore of Wigtown Bay, with spectacular views too good to be missed. Some road walking

Distance:	3 ½ miles/5.8km
Time:	2 hours
Map:	OS Landranger 83
Terrain:	Easy walking all the way.

11

Wood of Cree nature reserve

Park in the largish area opposite the entrance to the trail, grid ref. 381708—this is easy to miss and is on the north-west side of the cattle grid sign. The Wood of Cree lies on the east bank of the River Cree 4 miles north of Newton Stewart. It is reached by the minor road from Minnigaff to Glentrool, or from the A714 just south of Bargrennan.

Wood of Cree nature reserve is on the lower slopes of the Galloway hills, overlooking and including the marshes of the River Cree. The river in this area is slow moving and is known as the Loch of Cree. Its waters often flood the low-lying marshes. The oak woodland is one of the largest and

Waterfall on Cordorcan Burn, Wood of Cree

best examples of ancient woodland in southern Scotland. In early spring the woodland floor supports primroses and dog violets, to be followed by bluebells and wild garlic. In high summer cow wheat flowers between bilberry loaded with berries, luxuriating beneath the oaks. Tawny owls, buzzards and great spotted woodpeckers are residents of the wood and are joined by summer migrants, which include pied flycatchers, wood warblers, redstarts and tree pipits. The woodland trail is one mile and this can be extended to include the scrubland trail, making a walk of 2 miles. Along the way, plaques detail points of interest.

1. Cross the narrow road and continue up the good track. Go through the gap beside the gate, with the Cordorcan Burn to your right, dancing downhill through its water-scoured cleft. Where the track divides take the right fork; this brings you close to a pretty fall on the burn. Here you might see coal tits, goldcrests, blue tits, great tits and, in summer, wood warblers. Go on through coppiced oak and

Walk 11

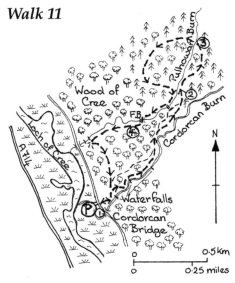

Pied flycatcher

hazel. These provided straight poles for pit props, fencing, cotton bobbins and firewood. Charcoal was produced for smelting locally mined lead. A plaque tells you that the wood has been actively managed since 1670. It was completely felled after the first world war so all the poles are over 80 years old but the root system is probably hundreds of years old.

41

2. Go on along the scrubland trail through an area that once was farmed and grazed by sheep and cattle. In 1976 the whole area was planted with dense conifers but since the establishment of the reserve, in 1984, the majority of conifers have been removed to create a mixture of wooded habitats, which include broadleaved scrub, scattered mature oak and some stands of sitka spruce and larch and plenty of bracken. The track winds steadily left.

3. Follow the arrows, directing you left, off the track, along a pleasing narrow reinforced path. It takes you over a small stream past several ancient crab apple trees. Then you pass into denser woodland to go by an 'erratic', a huge boulder carried a distance by a vast ice sheet and deposited here when the ice melted at the end of the last ice age. Go through the gap in the wall into oak woodland to come to the side of a hurrying burn. Follow the white arrow to walk on, with a stream to your left. Ignore the first sturdy footbridge (crossed if completing the woodland walk only) and go over the next one to continue along a railed way.

4. Then the path descends to come beside a stream on the right. Here an arrow directs you to a viewpoint and a seat overlooking Loch Cree. Return to the path and continue on to join a track. Bear right. One hundred yards along the path merges with your outward track. Go on descending to return to the car park.

Practicals

Type of walk: Easy walking over unobtrusive reinforced paths and tracks. Extremely well planned for maximum enjoyment of the woodland and the burns. Lots of small information boards and well waymarked.

Distance: 2 miles/3km
Time: 1 hour
Map: OS Outdoor Leisure 32

12

Loch Trool

Park in a small parking area close to Bruce's Stone, Glen Trool, grid ref. 415804, where there are toilets. The parking area is in Galloway Forest Park and is reached by a right turn at Bargrennan off the A714, 8 ½ miles from Newton Stewart or, 21 miles south from Girvan.

Bruce's Stone. A huge boulder standing high on a rough bluff commemorates the battle of Glen Trool. The eminence looks across Loch Trool to where, on 31 March 1307, 300 Scots led by Robert Bruce enticed an English force of 1500 men, many on horseback, into an ambush. The Scots rolled boulders down the steep slopes, pitching men and horses into the water. Archers picked off the survivors as they fled down the lochside. Bruce's final victory over the English came on the 24 June 1314, giving independence to the Scots.

Martyrs' Tomb, Caldons Camp Site. The tomb is found a short distance into Caldons Wood. The walled enclosure commemorates the death of six convenanters, put to death in sight of their wives

Loch Trool

and families, in January 1685. Robert Patterson (1712–1800), often called 'Old Mortality', dedicated his life to the maintenance of this and other Covenanter memorials.

1. Just beyond the toilets, follow a narrow path, leading off right from the main track, through heather and young birch, to Bruce's Stone, where you will want to linger. As you go look and listen for the first of the many wrens to be encountered on this walk. A similar path returns you to the main track. Turn right and follow the way as it descends in the direction of the loch. Go on to cross the fine bridge (built 1851) over the cascading Buchan Burn and continue on through scattered birch, hawthorn, willow and oak. Cross a bridge over the Gairland Burn and press on through more pleasing woodland. Ignore the track, ahead, to Glenhead farm and stroll the reinforced track as it bears right and brings you to a sturdy wooden footbridge over Glenhead Burn to reach a four-armed signpost.

2. Go ahead over the stile to walk the Southern Upland Way in a westerly direction. Pass below overhanging larch, on your left, with a fine view over open slopes to the hills, to your right. The path climbs steadily, rocky in places, and then descends with views of the loch ahead. Pass the plaque at the site of the battle of Glen Trool. The switchback path continues delightfully on.

3. The main path, waymarked, climbs through mature Scots pine, but you may prefer to take a narrow path, off right, that leads down to the lochside and then continues closer to the water's edge. This fine way provides many pleasing views. Both routes eventually join and the lovely way, with glorious glimpses of the loch reflecting the hillside above, continues. The track finally climbs a slope and bears right to a kissing gate above Caldons camp site.

4. Beyond walk through a birch glade, with scattered oaks. Join a reinforced track and walk left. Cross a metalled bridge giving access to a large open area. Bear right and follow the way left into a smaller open area where in high summer hardheads attract innumerable peacock butterflies. Go with the path to pass the campsite toilet block and continue with the stream on your left. Cross the footbridge and bear right. To see the Martyrs' tomb, continue ahead when the track turns right to the main bridge into the site. Turn left as directed

Walk 12

and follow the path and then duckboarding to reach the tomb. Return to the main bridge and cross the burn again.

5. Beyond, bear right through a small parking area to join a waymarked footpath, one of the forest trails, which takes you through a large cleared area. At the time o f writing, felling of the trees had opened up a good view of the lower end of the loch. The path leads you into woodland.

6. Look for the waymark away to your left that directs you left and then right to climb steadily through the forest trees, away from the loch. It continues beside a burn, which you cross to reach a forest road. Turn right to return to the car park.

Practicals

Type of walk: This is a circuit of Loch Trool along mainly forest paths, well waymarked. Choose a fine day to enjoy the views.

Distance:	5 miles/8km
Time:	3–4 hours
Maps:	OS Landranger 77
Terrain:	Some steady climbing required on the south side of the loch. Three quarters of a mile walk along a metalled forest road. Expect some of the paths to be muddy and quite difficult after rain.

13

Buchan Burn, Buchan Hill, Loch Neldricken, Loch Valley, Gairland Burn

Park as for walk 12

Buchan Hill walk. This is a great walk but not one to be attempted in the mist—the views are too good to miss. From its delightful summit (1605 ft/493m) and its two lesser cairned humps, count the number of lochs you can see and, from your map, try to name the surrounding hills. The way up, steepish in parts, is generally dry, with few distinct paths. Beyond the top, the route continues, pleasingly, along a grand extended rocky ridge to come to a boundary wall. The pathless descent, beside the wall to Loch Neldricken, is over tiresome tussock grass, which raises itself in ankle-wrenching clumps above sodden ground. The return is made along clear paths and tracks but after rain these can become waterlogged.

Loch Valley

Mountain hare

Falls of Buchan Burn. The cart track from Bruce's Stone car park leads downhill to the bridge over the splendid impetuous burn. Then as you climb the open fell, to the right of the burn, approach its magnificent ravine (with care) to see the mountain stream racing far below. It tumbles in foaming falls and through deep dark pools as it passes below oaks, between moss covered boulders, splashing lush ferns and liverworts as it goes.

White hare. The hare changes the hue of its coat at the beginning of winter but never the black tips of its ears. It lives above the line of cultivation and feeds on grass—and its roots—and on lichen. It makes its 'form' in rock crevices and among stones, where it is sheltered from the sight of birds of prey.

Walk 13

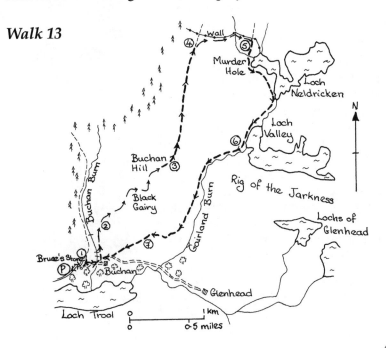

1. From the car park, walk on and then descend the steeply, winding, reinforced track to cross the bridge over Buchan Burn. A few yards on climb a rickety stile on the left. Follow the arrow that directs you uphill, with the Buchan burn to your left. Go through a gate in the stone wall ahead and continue climbing up the steepish grassy slope to the top right corner to pass through the gate in the wire fence. Pause here to look down on Loch Trool.

2. Go on up, with a small stream to your right. Where it turns away right, look ahead and slightly right, to see the route continuing to Buchan Hill. Cross a mirey patch, step across another stream and aim for a grassy hollow, with a terrace-like trod sloping up out of it at the right end. Once at the end of the terrace, wind left and almost immediately right over a rough rocky area. Pause and look down right to see the Long Loch and the Round Loch of Glen Head below the hill of Craiglee. Here you might disturb a mountain hare.

Ahead you can see the subsidiary cairn of the hill. Stride over the fell to stand and try to name some of the hills. Beyond this cairn, descend a dip and climb the fairly clear path up to the summit. To your right you can now see, far below, much of your return route beside lochs and burns.

3. Follow the narrow path that winds to a third cairn on Buchan Hill, with the higher Benyellary to your left, seemingly just across the way. Continue on along a more distinct path, remaining on the ridge and heading for the slopes of Merrick. Stay with the ridge as it bears north-west, with Merrick now to your left and Loch Neldricken (far below) to the right. Carry on, steadily descending to the side of a wall that you can see running down the slopes, east, to the side of the loch.

4. Turn right before the wall and descend through the tussock grass to a steep rocky area. Here it is easier to bear right and

Bog asphodel and spagnum

then skirt round the outcrop. Carry on down through bracken to cross, on rocks, a lively stream and continue beside the wall to come to a huge boulder. This stands beside a distinct track.

5. Turn right and begin your walk above Loch Neldricken. Re-cross by more boulders the burn you crossed earlier. The path then descends to the edge of the water and takes you round what is called Murder Hole on the map—a small bay of deep water, which is reputed never to freeze. The path then moves away from the water's edge and climbs a small promontory. Press on along the path well above the loch shore parallel with Mid Burn. This mountain stream descends in delightful cascades into a loch named Loch Valley. Look left as you progress to see it stretching away, eastwards, amid the lonely slopes.

6. Go on along the path that now keeps above the Gairland Burn. It then moves away from the burn, remaining high on the slopes before skirting a craggy knoll to meet a wall. Continue parallel with the wall on your left and watch for the grand view ahead of Loch Trool. Go through a gate in the wall and follow the way over the open grassy hillside to pass a lone rowan on the left.

7. Cross a stream and then go by another rowan to meet the wall again. Go through another gate in the boundary ahead. Continue on with a wall to your left. Clamber down a steepish rocky area and then pass left through the wall by a gate. Carry on along a wide grassy swathe, descending steadily to the track taken at the outset. Turn right to ascend to the car park.

Practicals

Type of walk: This is a good trek for experienced fell walkers. Choose a fine day, don't rush. Enjoy the magnificent views as you go.

Distance: 7 miles/11.2km
Time: 4–5 hours
Map: OS Outdoor Leisure 32
Terrain: Few paths. After rain or snow the trods can become very wet especially on the path beside the lochs.

14

Talnotry, The Grey Mare's Tail burn and Murray's Monument

Park in the small parking area at the foot of the Grey Mare's Tail burn to the east of Murray's Monument, grid ref. 490721. This lies beside the A712 (The Queen's Way), 11 miles west of New Galloway.

Grey Mare's Tail. The burn gathers its water on the Fell of Talnotry to descend in a series of delightful cascades. It then plummets in long white waterfalls, which give the burn its name, into the Palnure Valley. The valley has long been a route through the Galloway Hills, passing between the Fell of Talnotry and Cairnsmore of Fleet. Bronze Age man hunted deer by driving them through the valley and trapping them as the vale narrowed. Part of this walk is along a track, the Old Edinburgh Road, once used by pilgrims on their way to Whithorn, where St Ninian is believed to have founded the first Church of Scotland in about AD 397.

Murray's Monument. Alexander Murray, a self-taught linguist, was born in 1775 at nearby Kitterick Cottage. His father was a shepherd and Alexander, at the age of ten, was employed as a shepherd's boy. By very hard work he taught himself Latin, Greek,

Hebrew and French and in 1794 his achievements gained him admission to the University of Edinburgh, where he learnt several eastern dialects. In 1812 he became Professor of Oriental Languages at Edinburgh University but, alas, he did not long enjoy his appointment, dying in his late thirties of

Goldcrest

tuberculosis

50

Before you set off on the main walk you may wish to stroll out of the back of the car park to see Buck Loup, a fine waterfall lower down the burn than the Grey Mare's Tail waterfall and often mistaken for it.

Walk 14

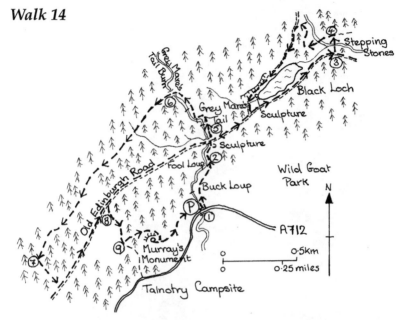

1. Walk a few yards east along the A712 to cross the bridge over the Grey Mare's Tail Burn. Leave the road, left, by a waymarked post immediately beyond the bridge. Climb the narrow grassy path through bracken towards a plantation. Gradually heather replaces the bracken. As you go you may wish to take one of the narrow paths, to the left, to glimpse the charming falls where the burn descends the steep slopes. Scramble up through rocks, or wind right around the craggy outcrop, to come to a waymarked post.

2. Here, pass through the wall on the left and walk towards several old sheep pens, where a series of stone heads have been sculpted by an artist into the walls of the pens. This and other work is part of a three year programme managed by Dumfries and Galloway Arts Association and initiated in 1997 by Forest Enterprise to celebrate Galloway Forest's 50th anniversary as a park. Continue on, following the waymarks, to the Old Edinburgh Road, a track,

The Grey Mare's Tail, Talnotry

C.M.Isherwood

where you turn right. Head on towards Black Loch. Dawdle beside the pretty stretch of water and then go through a gate and continue on for a short distance to a cycle waymark, which stands on the right.

3. Take the easy-to-miss footpath on the left opposite the post (for cyclists), through the trees to come to the side of the outlet stream from the loch. Cross by convenient stones. (If the burn is in spate you may have difficulty and have to return along your outward track beside the loch). Walk ahead through marshy woodland

towards a waymark that stands at the top of a slope leading to a grassy forest track.

4. Turn left and continue to cross another small stream on larger boulders (again this may be troublesome if in spate). Look upstream to see a fine waterfall. The continuing way swings right and then left and finally climbs steadily to a forest road, where you turn left. Follow this gently downhill to walk opposite to where you walked earlier beside Black Loch. Pause to enjoy another piece of contemporary art, an unusual tall conical construction, named 'Eye', covered with a mosaic of small pieces of stone. Walk on, retracing a short length of your earlier way along the Old Edinburgh Road to come to the side of the Grey Mare's Tail burn once again.

5. Do not cross but turn right. Follow a clear narrow path beside the hurrying water to stand below the tempestuous waterfall (50ft) as it leaps over the rim of a rocky amphitheatre and down into a seething brown plunge pool. Here you have a choice. You can return to the Old Edinburgh Road and walk on. Or, if you want a much more challenging walk, you should continue on up a stepped way. A little scrambling leads to where the path winds left through tall conifers. More steps take you on up, with strands of wire between you and the ravine. Stay with the fence to your left and follow it as it winds right to pass more cascades. Go on through a pleasing open area to cross the once turbulent burn, now a quiet mountain stream, by a bridge.

6. For the next three-quarters of a mile a narrow distinct path climbs and then continues as a high level way between conifers. This traverses peat. The way is frequently very wet and heavy going and you should allow plenty of time for this section. (Forest Enterprise has no plans to improve this path because of the near impossibility of getting vehicles and materials to this section of the forest.) When the path moves out into a clear-felled area you have a grand view of Murray's monument. Then the way widens and becomes reinforced for a short distance, with a good view ahead of Cairnsmore of Fleet.

7. Follow the path as it descends and winds round on itself, with a wall to the right. Then it drops down steeply and is again extremely wet and rough underfoot. It leads to the forest road (Old Edinburgh Road), where you turn left. You are now walking parallel to and

in the opposite direction from the high level path you have just come along.

8. After a quarter-of-a-mile, look out for the arrowed post, directing you right down a slope on a wide grassy track. (If you have decided to give the higher path a miss and have continued along the track remember to turn left at this point.) The track curves easily left and then begins to descend gently to a green post with a yellow band.

9. Turn left here to ascend a delightful needle-strewn track into the woodland that traverses the hillside. Follow it out into the open and into a hollow. Go with the track as it curves round and joins a stone surfaced path. Turn left and climb steps cut into rock to stand by Murray's monument and enjoy the splendid view. (This route from the marker post was a new track when walked by the author and one for which Forest Enterprise thought it better to use its limited resources rather than on the higher path described above.) Return down the steps to the good path and go on downhill to the car park.

10.Three-quarters of a mile along the A712 in the direction of New Galloway, a signpost points right to the cottage where Alexander Murray was born.

Practicals

Type of walk: The high-level path makes for a challenging walk. The route to the Grey Mare's Tail Burn waterfall is a small challenge in comparison but, even so, care should be taken.

Distance:	5 miles/8km
Time:	2–3 hours
Map:	OS Outdoor Leisure 32, Landranger 77
Terrain:	The path to the monument is easy to walk and so is the Old Edinburgh Road. All other paths are rough.

15

St John's Town of Dalry

The village has no car park and cars are usually left along the side of the quiet wide Main Street, grid ref. 622813. The village is reached by the A702, A762 and A713.

St John's Town of Dalry. This delightful village, situated above the Water of Ken, is called Dalry for short. It takes its name from the Knights of St John, an order originally formed to assist pilgrims on their way to Jerusalem. A Knights unit, founded in Dalry, helped pilgrims who were making their way from all parts of Scotland to Whithorn Priory.

John the Baptist's Chair, Dalry

Wildlife. In the summer months the shingle banks of the Water of Ken are busy with common sandpipers, grey wagtails and oyster catchers. Where there is sufficient cover mallard and tufted ducks raise their broods. In September hundreds of wildfowl arrive from the Arctic to spend the winter in the Ken Valley. Greylag geese graze in the fields beside Dalry.

Walk 15

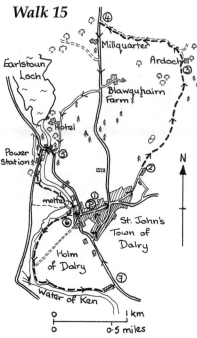

1. Walk up Main Street. Ignore the first left turn, the B7000. Go on to the top end of the village until you reach a Southern Upland Way (SUW) signpost, which stands on the right side of another left turn. Look for the pleasing primitive stone seat, known as John the Baptist's Chair, beside the SUW signpost—the logo on the latter has the carved outline of a thistle. Follow the SUW arm directing you northwards along the left turn, a 'no through road'. Where the road swings left, go on ahead to walk a reinforced track, with houses on either side.

2. Pass Townhead Cottage and follow the clearly waymarked rising track out into gently rolling open country. Enjoy the fine views as you go and continue to a ladderstile that takes you over the wall on the left. Beyond the stile, follow the waymarks taking you, by a clear path, across wild moorland. Go on over the sometimes wet way, heading in the direction of Ardoch farm, which you can soon see ahead, nestling among trees.

3. Go through a gate and on along a track, keeping to the left of the farm. Where the SUW swings right, leave it to follow the farm access track and stay with it as it winds left to walk to the road. To your left is Cairnsmore of Dee and, ahead, the Rhinns of Kells.

4. Turn left and go on to pass Millquarter farm. Just after the signpost for Blawquhairn farm, turn right. Down below to the right is Earlstoun Loch. Continuing on this delightful way, you pass a seat where you may wish to pause and enjoy the pleasing view. Go on past Milton Park hotel.

5. At the A-road, cross and turn right to walk the bridge over the Water of Ken. Just beyond, wind left to pass the water power station and then take, on the left, another part of the signposted SUW.

Pass through broom and gorse and continue on the well waymarked path along the riverbank. Cross the suspension footbridge. At its end, walk left to see the SUW information shelter. Beyond the shelter rises Dalry Motte, a flat-topped earth mound where once stood a 12th century castle.

6. Opposite the shelter, climb the stone stepped stile into the burial ground of the church to see the engraved horizontal grave slab of two Covenanters shot in 1684. Walk round to the far side of the pinnacled church to the ruined crow-stepped Gordon Aisle, part of the medieval church that once stood on this site. It was the former burial ground of the Gordons of Lochinvar. Leave the churchyard by the same stone stile and turn left and left again, before the bridge, to walk below the wall of the church. Carry on ahead along the path, or the floodbank, to stroll for 1 ½ miles around the Holm of Dalry and beside the lovely Water of Ken. The way winds steadily left, following the curve of the river. At a reinforced track, turn left to join the A713.

7. Stride left for 400 yds, facing oncoming traffic, to take, on the right, Kirkland Street. Climb steadily to pass Dalry school and, beyond, turn left to walk through the gate to reach the Main Street and your car.

Practicals

Type of walk: This varied walk, starting from a delightful village, takes you over moorland, along lanes shaded by deciduous trees and around a delightful curve of the Water of Ken.

Distance:	7 miles/11.2km
Time:	3–4 hours
Map:	OS Landranger 77
Terrain:	Some walking along quiet minor roads. Take care on the A713—you use it only for a short distance, but the traffic travels fast.

16

Dromore to Mossdale

A linear walk from the Visitor Centre at Dromore to Mossdale, using the Route of the Old Railway Track (two cars required).

This walk uses two cars, one taking you to the start and the other awaiting you at the end, but if this is not possible you could do the walk on two days, starting from either end and returning when you are roughly halfway. There is no public transport.

Leave the second car in a grassy parking area close to the old station at Mossdale, grid ref. 661706. To reach this take the A762 north from Laurieston for four miles. Just before the post office and village store take a track on the right, between the A-road and a B-road. It makes an acute right turn. The parking area lies on the left along the track. Then return, with all your walking gear, to Gatehouse of Fleet and continue north along the very pleasant B796. After six miles turn right to follow the signs for the parking area at the Visitor Centre at Dromore, grid ref. 555638.

1. From the centre—a small cottage and museum, with a dramatic backdrop of the Clints of Dromore—stroll on along the good track towards the magnificent rose-coloured viaduct. As you approach

you can see its twenty pillars are constructed of brick and its arches of stone. It curves gracefully as it strides the Big Water of Fleet, the surging burn giving its name to the viaduct. Pass under the bridge and press on. Ignore the first right turn and continue into coniferous forest to take the next right.

2. Go on through the trees to cross the bridge over the pretty burn and at a T-junction take another right turn. Follow this as it winds left and climbs steadily through a vast area of clear-felled forest. The way eventually continues parallel with the railway track that runs along on your right, obscured by lush vegetation. Eventually the forest track and the old railway line unite, the latter coming in on your right. The way then goes on as a forest road, using the route of the trackbed. Look left here for a fine view of Cairnsmore of Fleet.

Walk 16

3. The way passes through a clear-felled area and then an open area, with rocky outcrops, where the conifers are planted well back. Go through a cutting and follow the curving way. Pass between abutments of an old bridge and stroll on to where the forest road curves left and you can see the embankment that carried the railway line stretching dramatically ahead. Do not be tempted to go on along this high level way as there is no way to cross the Little Water of Fleet. Instead remain on the forest road as it soon curves right, running parallel with the embankment, to a tractor bridge, which you cross.

4. Continue on the curving way to come to a fine stone arched sheep

Goldeneye

creep, through which animals could pass safely below the railway line. At this point turn left, off the forest road, to walk the trackbed; from now onwards it remains as a disused railway line and has not been converted to a forest road. Pass between rock faces with lush beds of mosses, liverworts and lichens. Go through a cutting and press on. Look for reed buntings in the willows colonising the drainage ditches beside the track. At a very wet area, look for a small path taking you up on the left bank.

5. Ahead you can now see the heather-clad Airie Hill. Then the conifers cease on the right and bleak wild moorland stretches away up the slopes of Laughenghie Hill. On the left the conifers 'step back' and you have your first glimpse of the glorious Loch Skerrow. Go through a sliding gate and walk on the delightful heather-bordered way, with scattered rowans edging the track. In spring, autumn and winter, pause and look for goldeneye fishing and idling on the lovely waters, their large white eye patch and large heads making them easy to identify.

6. Carry on to pass the remnants of atmospheric Skerrow Halt, still with the rotting timbers of its platforms in place and a small ruined hut set back from the track. Walk on to cross the sturdy tractor bridge over the Grobdale Lane—'lane' here used as a name for a burn that is nigh on impossible to wade. Pass through the next gate.

7. The track now passes through a gentler area, Lyons Wood, with scattered deciduous trees, rocky outcrops and bracken clad hillocks. Bog myrtle grows along the drainage ditches. Beyond the next gate you can glimpse Stroan Loch. As you walk on look right to see the white buildings of lonely Airie, sheltered by a cluster of conifers, and with a view down towards the waters of the loch. Continue on to a cattle grid, and pause here before you cross Stroan viaduct for an extensive view of the loch and, to the left, the lovely Black Water of Dee, racing away from the loch, its banks lined with birch and its progress hindered by boulders.

8. Stroll on through a deep cutting where the towering sides are a botanist's paradise. And then, after passing through a small

deciduous woodland, the track takes you out into what appears to be more open moorland. Alas this vast area, on either side, is closely planted with tiny trees. Continue on, enjoying the pleasing view ahead of the Ken Valley. Then pass under a bridge and, just beyond, to the left, is the parking area of your second car.

9. All that remains is to drive back to Dromore to pick up your other vehicle.

Viaduct over the Big Water of Fleet

Practicals

Type of walk: A very satisfactory walk through remote, varied and often austere countryside.

Distance:	8 ½ miles/13.5km
Time:	4 hours. Add time to get vehicles in place.
Map:	OS Landrangers 83 and 77
Terrain:	Level all the way. It is hard walking on the granite clinker of the trackbed.
NB:	You might wish to do the walk in the reverse, where the views ahead are more dramatic, but in a westerly wind you will prefer the route above.

17

Carstramon Wood

Park in a layby, grid ref. 589603, in the narrow lane that runs along the west side of Carstramon Wood. To reach this leave Gatehouse of Fleet by the fell road to Laurieston and, after three-quarters of a mile, take the minor that leads off left.

Parliament. A large oak tree, to the left and behind the explanatory board of the Scottish Wildlife Trust, has always been known as 'Parliament'. The tree was, and still is, a natural meeting place for those who live in the valley.

Carstramon Wood. The wood is a site of ancient woodland. The oak trees you see on the walk were planted about 200 years ago, using English acorns.

Flora and Fauna. In spring the woodland is alive with summer migrants, for example, pied flycatcher, wood warbler, redstart and willow warbler. In May the

Bluebells

woodland floor is carpeted with a magnificent display of bluebells. The presence of these lovely flowers is a good indicator that this area has been wooded for very many years.

Charcoal Burning Platforms. At least five platforms exist below Doon Hill. These lie close to the track, which was constructed for extraction of timber and charcoal. Oak was cut near to the platforms and converted into charcoal to be used for smelting iron, brass and copper. It is estimated that this activity took place for about 100 years from 1830. Wood was used to supply a bobbin mill and a small wood-products business in Gatehouse of Fleet until 1931.

NB Please remain on the footpaths through the wood.

1. Walk up the path behind the information board. At the waymarked Y-junction take the right branch. Continue on climbing and, at the next two Y-junctions, take the right branches. Walk on below Doon Hill, rising on your left. Descend gently to a bench seat, which stands just below one of the flat raised platforms, and then go on down the path to see another.

2. Return back up the path to the waymarker and continue ahead through the ancient woodland. Step across a well culverted stream. Just beyond, turn right and continue gently to cross another small stream. At the next path, turn right and follow the path out of the wood onto open moorland.

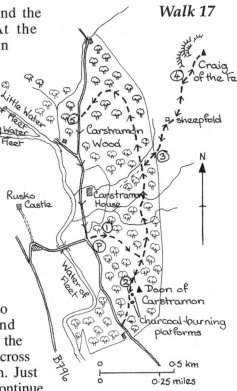

Walk 17

63

3. Bear half left and pass through bracken covering a small hillock and then find your way across a wet area, aiming for the rocky 'bun-shaped', heather-clad hill, an outlier of Castramont, rearing up beyond gentle slopes. Join a grassy path that leads to a sheep pen beside the boundary wall. Walk right along the wall for a few yards to go through a metal gate. Several paths, beyond the gate, lead up over the open fell towards the hill. All of these come close to each other and one leads you upwards to the cairned summit. Pause here to enjoy the magnificent view of Cairnsmore of Fleet and the valley of the Fleet.

4. Return by the same route to the access gate into Carstramon Wood and continue through the trees to the waymark. Turn right and walk on to cross a small stream. The path leads you through oak woodland and gently descends. At the next waymark and seat, turn right and carry on down, eventually through ash; both ash and oak have been coppiced at some time. The path leads you to the minor road.

5. Turn left to walk the pleasing way, enjoying the rich vegetation, with bluebells stretching away on either side and birdsong filling the air. Go quietly and watch for roe deer. As you near the start of the walk, look right to see, through the trees, the 16th century Rusko Castle, an austere simple rectangular tower house.

Practicals

Type of walk: A delight at all times but especially so when the bluebells are in flower. Please stay on the footpaths.

Distance:	2 ½ miles/4km
Time:	2 hours
Map:	OS Landranger 83
Terrain:	Easy to walk well waymarked paths in Carstramon Wood. Steady climb, wet at first and then dry to the hill top.

18

Loch Whinyeon

Park beside the signpost for Loch Whinyeon, grid ref. 610606, on the right (east) side of the fell road from Gatehouse of Fleet to Laurieston

NB The walk beyond the gate is over rough fell and is the breeding site of many ground nesting birds. Walkers are asked to avoid this area from April until July. Dogs must be on close lead.

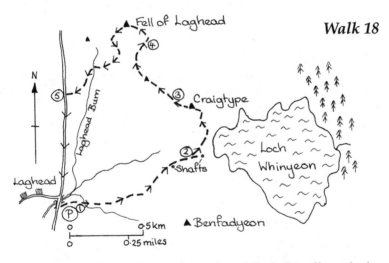

Walk 18

1. Stride the path as directed by the signpost. Climb the stile and take the right branch of the path. After continual but steady climbing along the clear path, go on ahead towards a conical cairn. Press on through banks of heather to come to a seat, with a delightful view of the quiet waters of the loch. It is surrounded on three sides by moorland and hills and on the fourth by a dramatic backcloth of the conifers of Glengap Forest.

Loch Whinyeon

2. Bear left, clockwise around the loch, coming close to a boundary wall. Pass through a gate and turn left to climb a steep gully between outcrops to achieve a small cairned summit, where grouse call and then fly off. The view is spectacular.

3. Follow a tractor-wheel rutted track as it winds left and then swings right, remaining on high ground. Look north across a lower marshy area (col) to see the cairn on Fell of Laghead, the high point of your walk. Cross the lower area at its narrowest part—here the vegetation has been cut to encourage the regeneration of the heather.

4. Climb the Fell of Laghead, bearing right and then left to ease the gradient. As you ascend you lose sight of the cairn but begin to have, to your right, a good view of the loch. Go on upwards to the cairn and enjoy the extensive view. Then leave the top, left (south), to look down on the low marshy ground crossed earlier, and a good grassy track leading right to the fell road. Descend the slopes and join the track to walk right.

5. At the road, turn left to return to the start of the walk.

Practicals

Type of walk: A pleasant moorland route to a remote loch, with a return over rough fell slopes and tops.

Distance:	2 ½ miles/4km
Time:	1 ½ hours
Map:	OS Landranger 83
Terrain:	Clear path to loch, muddy in parts after rain. The pathless way over the marshy col can be wet.

19

Gatehouse of Fleet and Anwoth

Park in the free car park, grid ref. 600563, at Gatehouse of Fleet, close to the police station and the tourist information centre. To reach the small town, leave the A75 by the B796, just after crossing the Water of Fleet.

Rutherford Monument, Gatehouse of Fleet

Gatehouse of Fleet. Once there was just a house on the road (or gait) to the bridge over the Fleet. Today there are many two-storey houses along the wide main street. Many are painted white, and by their brightness and cheerfulness, give a warm welcome to visitors. Dominating the pleasing shops of the elegant large village is a splendid granite clocktower, built in 1871. At that time Gatehouse was a booming cotton town, with four mills, a brass foundry, a shipyard and several other industries. But these gradually closed as nearby larger towns took over. Today, close to the Water of Fleet, stand one of the remaining mills and two waterwheels, all pleasingly restored.

Samuel Rutherford (1600–1661) was the minister of Anwoth from 1627 until 1639. Previously he had been a

Professor of Humanity at Edinburgh but resigned in 1626 after an 'antenuptial irregularity'. In 1639 he became Professor of Divinity at St Andrew's and he wrote several religious books, including, in 1644, during the Civil War, *Lex Rex* [The law, the king], which argued for limitations on the idea of the Divine Right of Kings. In 1661, after the restoration of the monarchy, this book was burned by the hangman in Edinburgh and Rutherford was summoned for high treason. He received the summons on his death bed.

Cardoness Castle. From the top of the partly restored 15th century castle, a McCulloch stronghold, there are fine views over the delightful countryside around the Fleet estuary. A 17th century McCulloch was the last man to be executed by the Scots version of a guillotine, known as 'the maiden'. The castle is maintained as an ancient monument and there are details of opening times and entrance fee at the gate to the castle.

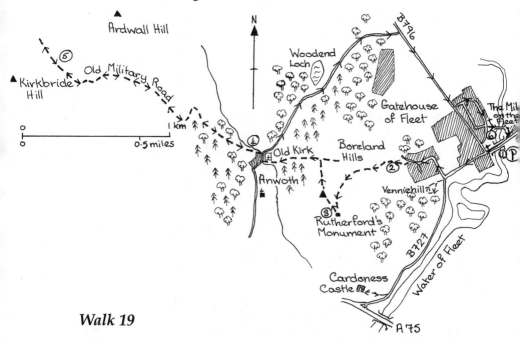

Walk 19

1. Walk back along the B-road (south-west) to cross the bridge over the Fleet. Cross to the right side of the road and, where the road makes a sharp left turn, look for the entrance gate leading, after a short climb, to the viewpoint on Venniehill. You might wish to

visit the hill for a fine aerial view of the spacious town in its woodland setting. On your descent turn left (or right if you decide not to ascend the hill) to follow a narrow road. It winds left and climbs uphill. Go past a seat on the left and continue on to go through a waymarked gate on your left. It is just before a cattle grid. Walk a delightful path, with a wall to the right and larches to the left. Pass through a deer gate and climb a stone-stepped stile.

2. Follow the path as it climbs right through scattered birch and hawthorn, passing a marker post with the outline of a monument on it. Continue upwards, staying parallel with a wall to your right. Then the trig point comes into view and next the monument. Follow the wall round as it winds left and then go through it to a stile into a rather wet area. Bear right and follow the clear path round left, cross a small stream and then take one of the paths ahead that lead up to the monument. From here you have a spectacular view of the Water of Fleet surging out into Wigtown Bay, and over the top of the trees you can spot Cardoness Castle.

The Samuel Rutherford Monument was erected in 1842. The plaque says that it was constructed

> in admiration of his eminent talent, extensive
> learning, ardent piety, ministerial faithfulness and
> distinguished public labours in the cause of civil and
> religious liberty.

3. Leave the monument and cross to the trig point to enjoy the view of the pretty valley of the Fleet. Go on ahead to descend a dip and then climb up the next hillock. Descend once more to a gate into mixed woodland. Follow the track downhill and emerge from the trees by a gate. Walk on, keeping to the left of the ruined Anwoth Kirk and kirkyard. After passing through two gates, join a narrow road. Turn right to go through the gate on the right to the cemetery. Enjoy its peaceful environs where, on a plaque, there are more details about Samuel Rutherford. The ruined kirk was in use until the early 1800s and then a new church was built a quarter of a mile to the south.

4. To extend this walk, bear right on leaving the gate from the cemetery, cross the lane and then bear left, beside a pretty cottage, to walk a gated track, the Old Military Road. This pleasing way (very muddy in parts in the winter and requiring wellington boots) takes you out into quiet countryside and you can walk along it for

as far as you wish. The road was built by the military in the 1740s, to help in the transport of the Royal Mail from Ireland after the post had arrived at Stranraer. The military were the only people who, at that time, had the equipment and manpower to construct such a lengthy route.

5. Return back along the Old Military Road. At the cottage at Anwoth, turn left and continue for nearly a mile along a delightful hedged lane to reach the B796. Turn right and walk on for a quarter of a mile to the start of the houses at Gatehouse of Fleet. Cross and take the first left beyond the fire station, called Fleetside. Follow the road as it soon bears right. Beyond the Roman Catholic church, go left over an open grassy area to dawdle across a long footbridge over the chattering Fleet. Here you might spot a white-bibbed dipper, bobbing on a midstream rock. The bridge gives access to another open area beside the restored mill with its waterwheels.

6. From here it is a short walk to the main street and the car park. A mile along the B-road, on your return to the A75, you may like to visit Cardoness Castle. The ruin is reached by flights of steps between steeply sloping lawns.

Practicals

Type of walk: The walk to the monument and trig point, and then the descent to the kirk, involves gentle climbs and descents through woodland and over heathery hillocks.

Distance: 3 ½ miles/5.6km plus the distance you walk along The Old Military Road.
Time: 2 hours
Map: OS Landranger 83
Terrain: Easy paths and tracks. The Old Military Road becomes excessively muddy at times.

20

Martyrs' Memorial and Loch Mannoch

Park in a layby on the west side of the narrow reinforced lane, which goes off left at the Y-junction a few yards north of Glengap farm, grid ref. 652596. The verge is reached by a B-road that heads north for 3 miles from Twynholm, by-passed by the A75.

Martyrs' Memorial. The memorial lies on the lower side of an isolated walled clump of scots pine and larch. It marks the place where, in 1685, several Covenanters were put to death for refusing to accept Charles II as head of the Church of Scotland. In 1861 about 10,000 people assembled here to commemorate the event and contribute to the cost of the memorial.

Walk 20

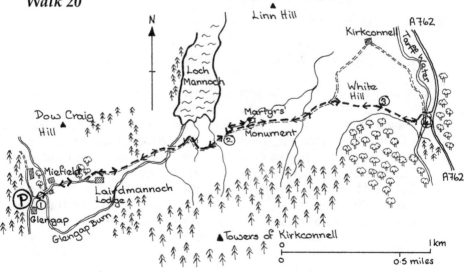

e.M.Isherwood

1. Return to the continuing metalled road just above the farm and walk left to cross Glengap Burn. Stroll on to pass between a house named Miefield on the right and the outbuildings on the left called Miefield farm. Where the track bears right to Lairdmannock Lodge, go on along the left branch to pass through a gate. Bear right to follow the track as it descends, with Loch Mannoch lying to your left. Here in high summer you might see a pair of stonechats, shepherding their young on the wire fencing. Cross the tractor bridge over a stream and look for dragonflies flitting above the surface of the water. Climb steadily up the track and, near the brow, look for the sliding bars—called a flake—in the fence on your left.

2. Go through, wind right and follow a faint sheep trod through a marshy glen to the Martyrs' memorial at the edge of a clump of trees. As this book went to press, the access was due to be improved. After your visit, return by the same route to go through the gate to rejoin the track and walk on (left), descending steadily to a cattle grid, with a gate beside it. Immediately beyond, the track veers sharply left and there is a 'Private, no entry' sign with a footpath sign directing you right. Walk the grassy way between two low hills and, once through the dip, descend, keeping to the left of some trees and rushes, to climb the stile in the wall.

3. Walk on, with a wall to your left, to the next stile. Beyond, turn left to walk a good track. Across the Kirkconnell Burn, in high summer, look for marsh ragwort, purple loosestrife, meadow sweet and valerian. Go through the gates across the track and turn right to cross the bridge over the burn, if you wish to join the A762.

4. As there is no suitable circular return route, retrace your steps on your outward walk.

Grey wagtail

Practicals

Type of walk: A linear walk through quiet moorland and pastures, on good tracks and paths, except for the approach to the memorial

Distance:	4 miles/6.5km
Time:	2 hours
Map:	OS Landranger 83
Terrain:	Easy walking generally.

21

Kirkcudbright

Leave your car in the Harbour Square car park, grid ref. 684512. It is built on a former dock, which was used by boats when the tide rose much higher on the River Dee, and later filled in.

Kirkcudbright. Pronounced Kircoobree. The name is believed to be a corruption of Kirk-Cuthbert, named after the saint who converted much of this part of Scotland to Christianity. The pretty town has the wide streets of the 18th century, with terraces of two-storeyed pastel-coloured houses and many flower beds. Overlooking the harbour is the forbidding ruin MacLellan's Castle. This 16th century tower house was built by Thomas MacLellan, whose family supported the Royalists in the Civil War. Eventually the MacLellans lost all their money, and by the middle of the 18th century the house was seized and the roof removed.

Cup-and-Ring marks, High Banks, Kirkcudbright

High Banks cup-and-ring markings. Here outcrops of rock are covered with puzzling carvings of cups, rings and spirals. Some archaeologists believe that these markings might have been used as a pre-historic system of waymarking. From each cup-and-ring marked outcrop there probably was a clear view over nearby ground to other markings in the area, delineating paths used by Neolithic and Bronze Age people to find their way when herding animals from the coast to higher ground.

Walk 21

1. From the car park, walk along St Cuthbert Street in the direction of MacLellan's Castle. Turn left into Castle Bank and then wind round left again into High Street, which is lined with fine Georgian houses. Cross over St Mary's Street and continue on up the sloping St Mary's Place. Go on up, bearing left to pass in front of several bungalows on the right. Turn right into Woodlands Avenue to see, ahead, steps leading into woodland beyond a notice board for Barhill Wood.

2. Wind left at the top of the steps through the deciduous bluebell woodland. At the forest road, turn right and walk on. Ignore the track coming up from the right and continue bearing left to a yellow-banded waymark. Here climb left through the lovely trees. Go on steadily uphill, following the waymarks. Look right through the

Foxglove

trees to see delightful rolling farmland. At a reinforced track, turn right to climb a ladderstile out of the wood and into sheep pasture.

3. Bear slightly left, following tractor wheelmarks, across a large pasture to a waymarked stile. Turn left to stroll a track to the road. (Note the waymarked entrance for your return.) Turn right to walk the narrow lane, from where there are pleasing views. Continue on the glorious way between hedgerows and under forest trees as the road winds and curves down towards the Buckland Burn. Ignore the turn, left, before the bridge and the right turn after the bridge, and go on. After a mile of road walking from the track, take the right turn, signposted High Banks, and carry on for half a mile up the rough, steadily ascending access track. Pass a cottage on the left and a ruined one on the right. Carry on to a ladderstile, on the left, immediately before the farmhouse and its outbuildings.

4. From the ladderstile walk ahead to climb a pasture (no path) to another stile over the wall. From here go on climbing steadily to come to the outcrop of rocks with their magic markings. Pause here to enjoy the superb view of Kirkcudbright Bay and listen to the songs of meadow pipit and skylark.

5. Return across the two pastures and turn right to descend the farm's access track. At the road, turn left and walk on to cross the bridge and go ahead along the winding lane to the waymarked track, on your left, which you noted earlier. Walk the track to climb the ladderstile on the right and cross the pasture, bearing slightly left, to the stile into the woodland once again. Walk ahead on the reinforced track. Go forward at the cross of tracks and follow the reinforced way. Continue along it as it swings left. At another cross

76

Red squirrel

of tracks go on left for another 25 yds and, at the waymark, turn right to walk a short path to a ladderstile into a pasture. Follow a grooved track that bears steadily left, to another ladderstile into the trees. Once beyond, cross a track and descend the path to the stile to Woodlands Avenue.

6. Walk downhill to St Mary's Street and turn right and cut across the pretty green beyond the church to return to the car park. Here leave yourself time to walk the few steps to the harbour and then bear left to see its quaint houses.

Practicals

Type of walk: After leaving the attractive town enjoy the delightful woodland walk before continuing along a quiet country lane. Climb the track to High Banks farm and then over the high pastures to the emotive curiously marked rocks.

Distance: 7 miles/11.1km
Time: 3 hours
Map: OS Landranger 83
Terrain: Generally easy walking.

22

Balcary Point

Park opposite the hotel at Balcary Bay, grid ref. 820495, reached by a narrow two-mile-long 'no through road'. This leaves the A711 at Auchencairn, a village south-west of Dalbeattie.

Balcary Bay. Sheltered by Balcary Hill, Balcary Bay lies in the south west corner of Auchencairn Bay. The latter has many deep tidal inlets and there is easy access from the Isle of Man—both facts which, in the past, made it ideal for smuggling. The house that is now Balcary Bay Hotel was built in the 18th century by three Manxmen, named Quirk, Clark and Crain, to aid their contraband business with the island, which has always had its own tax laws. The cellars were constructed to hide valuable illicit goods. Today, the hotel, with its glorious gardens and views, is a haven of peace.

Adam's Chair. The path descends from the cliffs of Airds Point to continue above a platform of wave-eroded rocks, named Adam's Chair. This is believed to be the lookout point of a smuggler of that name who signalled to ships, laden with contraband, that the coast was clear of customs and excise men for landing their cargo.

1. Walk on from the parking area to the end of a stone house and take, on your right, a well waymarked footpath. Continue for a few steps to a signpost directing you in the direction of Balcary Point. Here a notice reminds you of dangerous cliffs. Bear left to wind round the field edge. A few yards along, look left for a grand view of the bay and of the stake nets stretching out into the estuary to trap salmon on the flood tide. Stroll on to the kissing gate into deciduous woodland.

2. Walk the delightful way to pass the old boathouse, once a lifeboat station and now an attractive house. Here remain by the fence on your right. Cross a track and continue along a narrow path, beside

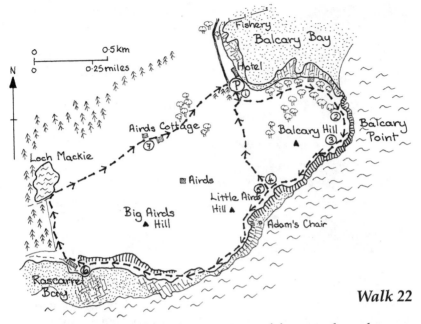

the fence, to emerge from the trees onto a rising way through gorse.
Continue on to the open cliff path. Pause here on the headland to
look back across the bay to Heston Island, with Criffel hill beyond.

3. Some walkers may wish to return at this point if they do not have
heads for heights. To continue, climb steeply up Balcary Hill to
round Balcary Point. Here the path comes very close to the edge of
spectacular, precipitous cliffs. Far below the tide licks jealously
around the feet of several dramatic stacks, one named Lot's Wife.
Sit on the bench seat to view this impressive stretch of the Solway
coast and to watch the cormorants, shags and rock doves fly in to
the rock faces and then out again. The path then descends to a
kissing gate, its flanking fence hanging in space over the cliff face.

4. Here you may prefer to return to the car park. To do so pass through
the gate, inland of the kissing gate. Turn left and go downhill by
the wall on your left. Go through the next gate onto a rough track.
A few yards down is a waymarked post on the right where you
leave the track and go onto the field. Cut across to the hedge corner.
Follow down beside the hedge on the left to a gate. Beyond walk
down a grassy hedged lane and follow it where it makes a right-
angled bend to the start of the walk.

Cliffs, Balcary Point

5. To continue the walk towards Rascarrel Bay, stroll on along the ascending path to Airds Point, where more lichen covered cliffs drop precipitously into the sea. Carry on above the wave-cut platform of Adam's chair and then follow the path as it drops to shore level, with shallow boulder-clay cliffs to the right and a wild rock strewn shore to your left. The path passes through banks of great reed, with clumps of meadow sweet and sea rocket.

6. Then you reach a row of wooden houses overlooking Rascarrel Bay. Follow the path that bears inland, winding behind the dwellings to a gate. Beyond, stride ahead, through gorse, to pass through another gate. Press on to a three-armed signpost beside the attractive reed-fringed, pretty Loch Mackie. Go through the kissing gate behind the signpost and turn right to stroll a farm track—delightful in dry weather but very muddy after rain.

7. Pass a derelict building on the left and then Airds farm on the right. Go on ahead along the track to where it ends at the car park.

Practicals

Type of walk: On paths through pleasing countryside and along fine cliffs, with grand views over the estuary of the Solway. Care should be taken on two parts of the cliff path which come very close to sheer drops.

Distance:	4 miles/6.4km
Time:	2–3 hours
Map:	OS Landranger 84
Terrain:	Good paths and tracks, with some climbing.

Screel Hill

Park in Screel Wood car park, grid ref. 799547. To reach this take the A711 south-west from Dalbeattie for five miles. Once past the signpost for Potterland, turn right for less than half a mile along a narrow lane to park on the left.

Screel Hill (1126ft/344m). Here heather-clad slopes rise dramatically above the hill's long skirts of conifers. Magnificent views to the Solway coast and of the Galloway Hills await you from the lesser summit and the top. The walk follows a well waymarked route, which rises steadily through the forest. The waymarks then direct you through banks of heather alongside the granite slopes; then you have to do a little scrambling onto the ridge. A pleasing track continues to the large cairned summit. The return is along forest rides and paths.

Walk 23

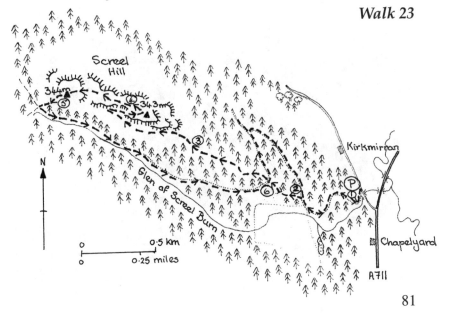

1. Follow the directions for the Screel on the notice board by the car park to continue along the track. When you reach a gate on the left onto open pasture and another notice board directing you along the forest road, look for the narrow path between the two and leading up the slope into the trees. Very shortly you spot the first waymark, a white-banded green post.

2. Continue on to come to the forest road. (Note this point for your return.) Cross and go on into an area of darker, more mature forestry, looking ahead to spot the rather widely spaced marker posts. Go through a small clearing and keep to the right of a seat—which, before the trees below matured, gave a good view. Go on, bearing steadily left with a steepish slope to your right, to a difficult to spot marker post by a fallen sitka spruce. Above is a series of railed fences which you pass . Beyond, the path becomes much clearer.

3. As you near the edge of the forest you have your first glimpse of the rocky ridge leading to the summit. A good waymarked path takes you on, out into the heather below flaring crags to your right. As the path begins to climb through a rocky cleft watch carefully for the easily-missed marker post that directs you sharp right and then back on yourself. Follow the waymarked zig-zags and then, with a short scramble, you arrive on the lesser summit, to enjoy the breath-taking panoramic view.

*The Screel
from
Almorness*

4. Turn left and follow the markers along the wide safe ridge to go across a dampish col. Then ascend to the cairned top, where you will want to idle.

5. To descend bear left, following the path, which drops rockily and steeply for a short distance to a waymark, on the right, just inside the forest. Walk on along a rather wet ride, with a wall to your right, to the next marker post that directs you left into the forest. The way continues, deep in needles underfoot and passing, delectably, below an arch of very tall Norway Spruce, to come to a forest road.

6. Bear left and look for the right turn (noted earlier), which is the start of the narrow path you took at the outset of the walk. This brings you back to beside the gate that leads onto a pasture and onto the forest road. If you miss the start of this path, continue on the forest road, following it where it winds right. This continues to the car park, passing the exit from the 'short cut' and the gate on the right.

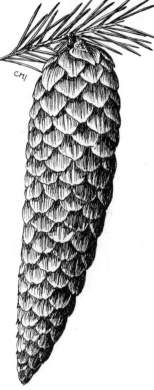

Norway spruce

Practicals

Type of walk: A pleasing, challenging walk to be enjoyed by all the family. Not to be attempted in the mist.

Distance:	4 miles/6.4km
Time:	2 ½ hours
Map:	OS Landranger 84
Terrain:	Good well graded paths and track, with one little stretch of scrambling.

Horse Isles Bay and White Port Bay

Park in the small parking area, on the left, before the stone entrance posts to the Almorness estate, grid ref. 823540. This lies 1 ½ miles along a narrow lane, south of Palnackie on the A711. If this area is full, return to Palnackie to park—the lanes from the village to the start of the walk are a delight.

Orchardton Tower. This tower house, 66ft high, is said to be the only circular one in Galloway. It was built in the late 1400s for John Cairns, laird of Orchardton. Climb the spiral stone staircase, with the help of a sturdy rope handhold, to pass through several rooms on the way to the roof-top balustrade. The tower is open to the sky and from it there are glorious views of Screel Hill and the lovely countryside around. (Visit on return to the A-road)

Reef. The rocks on the lower shore of White Port Bay are covered with a reef made by the honeycomb worm. These worms build tubes of sand grains bound together, in which they live. At high tide they put out a fan of tentacles to trap particles of food from the water, but at low tide the reef is exposed and the worms retreat inside. Sometimes the reef is destroyed by rough weather but usually regenerates in the same place.

1. Pass between the gate posts and go on along the narrow metalled lane, its banks in summer colourful with marsh woundwort, great burnet, honeysuckle, vetch, valerian and meadow-sweet. Very soon you can glimpse Orchardton Bay.

2. Beyond a cottage, the track, now no longer tarmacked, continues rising gently. Where the way swings left to Almorness House, pass through a gate with a stile beside it. Enjoy the pleasing view of Rough Firth.

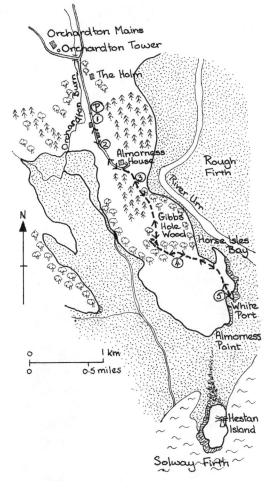

3. Ascend the easy track, with more glimpses of the firth and of the
   village of Kippford across the water. The track passes into mixed
   woodland and then emerges to an open area, on the right, where
   cattle graze. After passing two small pools the path begins to
   descend and passes through more woodland. It then curves east to
   go below some fine oaks.

4. Go through the kissing gate beside a padlocked gate to walk along
   the sandy shore of Horse Isles Bay, where you might see ringed
   plovers and oyster catchers. In mid-summer the shore line supports

rest harrow, sea club rush, sand sedge and sea couch grass. Here and there large patches of sea lavender brighten the drier areas.

5. At the end of the bay, wind round right to walk a grassy trod to cross a tractor bridge. Continue on through common reed and rush; if this area is too wet, use a narrow rough path, to the left, that runs through bracken and gorse. The routes soon unite. Go on and, suddenly, the vegetation opens out and White Port Bay lies below. Descend to the shoreline and dawdle on the lovely sandy beach. Perhaps you might spot the reef.

6. Return by the same route where, when you emerge from the woodland, you have fine views of the hills.

To visit Orchardton Tower, drive back along the narrow lane to take the first left turn. There is a good parking area. To reach the A711, continue on along the lane.

Orchardton Tower

*Honeysuckle and
rosehips*

Practicals

*Type of walk: Pleasing easily graded track takes you through
deciduous woodland to two sandy bays.*

Distance:	4 ½ miles/7.2km
Time:	2 hours or more depending on how long you stay on the sands.
Map:	OS Landranger 84
Terrain:	Very easy walking.

25

Rockcliffe Circular

Park in the National Trust car park at Rockcliffe, grid ref. 851536. This lies to the left just before you reach the seafront on the B-road, which leaves the A710 at Colvend.

Cow's Snout. South of Port o' Warren, the huge cliff, home to a cormorant colony, plunges steeply into the white topped breakers of an angry sea. The rose red of the cliff face contrasts pleasingly with the sulphur yellow of its coat of lichen, but much of it is overlaid with the white droppings of the cormorants. Their rough twig nests, lined with pieces of seaweed, are perched precariously on any small ledge. Pause awhile to watch the comings and goings of these handsome birds, masters of the air, as they wheel and float with outspread primaries, but who land, clumsily with legs outstretched.

Memorial to the schooner *Elbe*. This small cone-shaped stone monument lies on a flat sward to the sea side of the path, from where there is a fine view of Auchencairn Bay and Hestan Island. The plaque tells of the skill of the captain, Samuel Wilson of Palnackie, who in a storm on 6 December 1866, managed to land his crew and then back off the wooden boat from the rocks. It finally sank in Rascarrel Bay.

Memorial to the schooner Elbe *near Rockcliffe*

Stone age hill fort. As you near Rockcliffe, look down from the coastal path to see Castlehill Point, jutting out into the sea, with the grassy circular sward of the fort area atop. On exploring this look for a stretch of ancient wall and a ditch. There is an indicator board explaining the points of interest.

Nelson's grave. This is passed as you come close to the end of the coastal path. It has nothing to do with the famous admiral. The tombstone, in its low walled enclosure, commemorates Joseph Nelson—aged 69 years—who was drowned in January 1791 on a voyage from Whitehaven.

Walk 25

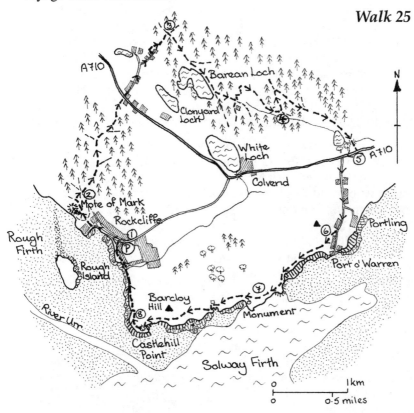

1. Turn left out of the car park and descend towards the bay. Over the pretty housetops of the village you can see Screel Hill. Unlike the next village, Kippford, Rockcliffe was never a haunt of smugglers but was a Victorian resort for sea bathing. Notice the blue lettuce

that flowers along the shore side of the road. Go past the toilets and then, at the end of the road, take the gated well signposted NT footpath to climb the Mote of Mark, a steep-sided, tree-skirted knoll. An information board tells of a stronghold occupied from the 5th to the 7th century AD and fortified by a rampart of stones and timber. From the top enjoy the superb view of Rough Island and Hestan Island, then descend to continue along the pleasant path.

2. At a cross of tracks, turn right and walk a glorious ride. Cross the Jubilee footpath and go into the forest to take the right branch. Ignore the next right turn and continue on to a sunny clearing with a seat. Press on in the direction of the signposted A710 and, as you go, look for siskins in the conifers along the ride. At the A-road, cross and turn left to take, on the right, a private road. Stride the lovely walled lane where, in autumn, gnarled sloe bushes are laden with fruit. Just before the end of the road, pass through the gate on the left, labelled 'access to the forest'. Wind right to a gate and, beyond, walk ahead, with the wall to the right, to descend gently to pass through a gate in the bottom right corner into Dalbeattie Forest.

3. Walk ahead to join the forest road, where you turn right. At the Y-junction take the right branch and go on past Barean Loch, with its water lilies; anglers fish here. Seats enable you to enjoy the view and, just beyond these, take the left fork. Continue gently uphill and, when you come to a cross of tracks, ignore the right turn to a building in the trees and take the left turn. It winds through an area of clear felling and then turns right and goes on to enter delightful mixed woodland—in summer the ride is a butterfly highway.

4. At the T-junction, turn left. In a short distance, where the track swings sharply left and uphill, walk right along a grassy ride. Go through the gate, beyond where you are asked to keep your dog on a lead. Join a reinforced access track. Continue ahead (walking right) along it for a fifth of a mile to join the A710.

5. Turn right and, 200 yards along, cross to take the left turn for Portling. Continue to the end of the metalled way, *Cormorant*

ignoring any left turns. Go on where the lane is reinforced, past a tearoom (which is open at weekends), and then descend steadily towards Port o' Warren. Watch for the sturdy, stepped, well signposted stile, just before a cottage, over the boulder wall on the right, directing you along the coastal path to Rockcliffe.

6. Beyond follow the path, which is fenced on the sea side, as it ascends between gorse. The lovely way goes on and on, with splendid views of the Firth. It crosses many walls by steps which are difficult to spot against the boulders at first but the path brings you unerringly to each one. The signposts along the way stand out clearly and reassuringly. And then the path begins to descend and the cliff edge becomes walled instead of fenced. Look back over the wall, where it turns left, to see the cormorant colony on Cow's Snout. Beyond it you can see Southerness lighthouse and across the Solway Firth to the Lake District.

7. Stroll on, keeping a lookout for the monument to the schooner, the Elbe, below the path. Wind on round Gutcher's Isle, overlooked by an ivy-clad ruin. Look down, with care, to the two tiny sandy inlets below. Take care as well as you wind round the next inlet, where the path squeezes between the wall and the cliff edge. Continue on, following the path as directed by large red arrows painted on prominent boulders. Look down on the hill fort at Castlehill Point and then go down, and then up, to it.

8. Continue on the path, following the clear signposting that takes you along the side of the estuary, past Nelson's grave to a road. Turn left and then right at the B-road to pass a teashop on your way to the car park on your right.

Practicals

Type of Walk. The walk starts along delightful woodland paths, and passes a quiet loch. It then returns by a magnificent coastal path from where there are outstanding views of dramatic cliffs and bird life.

Distance:	8 ½ miles/13.7km
Time:	5 hours
Map:	OS Landranger 84
Terrain:	Easy walking all the way.

26

Threave

Park in Threave Gardens main visitor centre car park, grid ref. 754605. To get there follow the signs for Threave Castle from the roundabout at the west end of Castle Douglas bypass (A75), and at the next roundabout turn left onto the B736. Where the B-road bears left, take the right turn for the gardens.

In 1948 Threave Estate was given to the National Trust for Scotland by Major Alan Gordon so that a wildfowl sanctuary might be established along the River Dee.

Threave Castle. It has been described as the most romantic place in Galloway. It was built in the late 14th century by the third Earl of Douglas, Archibald the Grim, and was later the stronghold of the Black Douglases. In 1455 the garrison surrendered to James II. In 1640 a Convenanter force laid siege to the castle, captured it

Threave Castle

and removed the roof and battlements. In the 18th century some work was done on the castle to turn it into a prison for French captives. In 1913 the owner, Edward Gordon, gave the property to the state. The ruin consist of a huge tower on an island in the River Dee. To reach it, ring the bell at the jetty and wait for the custodian to come and ferry you over. (For opening times phone Historic Scotland on 0131 668 8800.)

Walk 26

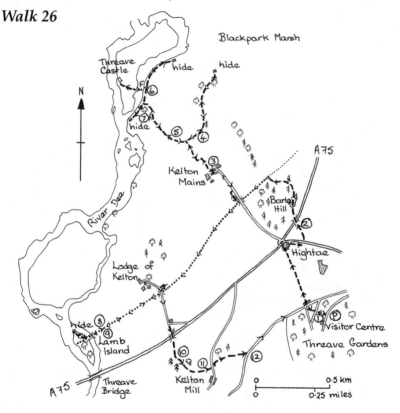

1. From the main car park walk down the waymarked grassy sward past the Belted Galloway 'cows' into the Estate Walk car park. Leave by the far kissing gate and, with care, cross the road. Walk ahead, between cottages, along a section called Hightae Strip. Go through a stile, cross a farm track and pass through a gate to continue on. Follow the yellow arrows to pass, on the left, Toll Booth cottage. Bear right along the access road until it comes close to the Castle Douglas road. Climb the steps ahead and for 100 yds walk the

railed way. Descend more steps to cross the road, again with great care, to walk the farm track opposite.

2. Continue onto a footbridge over the Castle Douglas by-pass. Head right to take a gate into a plantation of conifers and then follow the winding footpath, steadily downhill, with a fine view of Threave Castle, over the pastures. Go on to join the delightful route of the old Kirkcudbright railway line, where the last train ran in 1963. Walk on to pass under the stone railway bridge where you might wish to make a detour to visit Threave Castle and the three bird hides near to it. If so, leave the track by climbing steps on the right and then go on to walk the farm track to Kelton Mains farmhouse.

3. At the dwelling, wind left past the Bothy tearoom and then right to go through a gate to a fenced and walled track along the edge of a pasture. Follow it as the way turns left, then almost immediately right, to continue to a sign for the castle and for Blackpark marsh bird hide.

4. To reach the latter, turn right and climb two stiles to follow a pleasant path through woodland, waymarked with blue-banded wooden posts. As you pass through a clearing, look left for a glimpse of the castle. Continue on through more trees. At a junction you have a choice between two paths, both of which lead to hides overlooking the marsh. The hide reached by taking the right branch overlooks a small area. The left branch leads to a bridge over a wet area to a large sturdy hide from where you have an extensive view. Here, depending on the season, look for whooper swan, coot, mallard, widgeon, teal, pintail, tufted duck, goldeneye and dabchick.

5. Return by the same route to come to the signpost for the castle. Go on through the gate beyond and walk the fenced and gated way. Bear right towards the castle and walk the floodbank towards the jetty. Ring the bell for the custodian (great fun for youngsters) and cross the River Dee, which is wide here, to land on the island. Stroll the glorious green

Pintail

turf round the romantic ruin. Leave yourself time to cross the drawbridge and explore the well labelled and organised tower. Go to the other side of the island to see the surging river and the tiny harbour. Return by boat to the mainland.

6. From here you might wish to continue along the floodbank to another bird hide overlooking the Dee. Then return, with the castle to your right across the river. Where the path turns left a delightful short riverside walk goes on ahead, taking you to another hide which overlooks several small islands in the River Dee.

7. To continue the circular walk retrace your steps all the way to the railway track—don't miss the fenced path, to the right of the cattle grid, just before the railway bridge. Walk on along the track, a charming way in summer and a sheltered one in winter. Pass through several kissing gates to enter a cutting. Go through two gates very close together and continue under a railway bridge to dawdle on. Notice the wrought iron balustrade of the bridge. Carry on and as you go look left through the trees to see the fine Threave Bridge.

8. Cross the iron bridge ahead, onto Lamb island. Just beyond, leave the track, right, and descend steps into a small conifer plantation. A narrow path leads to another bird hide at the tip of the island— a magnificent spot overlooking a very wide reach of the river.

9. Retrace your outward route along the railway line. Go under the railway bridge and then leave the disused track. Wind round left on a new path to climb some wooden steps onto a road. Turn left, go over the railway bridge and walk on towards a single cottage. Here, keep straight ahead and go over a concrete bridge re-crossing the A75.

10.Just after a farm gate, a stile on the left allows you through a copse. At the far left-hand corner the route continues through a narrow double fence across the field before crossing a stile into a wider fenced area, with a young hedge planted in the middle.

11.Keep to the right of the strip, cross the footbridge over the Kelton Mill Burn and press on over a short stretch of boardwalk across marshy ground. Cross the minor road, with care, and walk up through the clear-felled conifer plantation opposite. Enjoy the marvellous views of Threave Castle with Carsphairn behind it and the Rhinns of Keld to the mountain's left.

12. At the far side of the clear-fell take a gate onto Rhonehouse road. Turn left and walk to the kissing gate leading to the car park (taken earlier). It is now on your right just beyond the end of a beech hedge over the wall, at the right side of the road. Go through and return to where you have parked.

Willow tit

Practicals

Type of walk: This delightful low level walk takes you through farmland, comes close to marshland, goes along an old railway line and onto two magical islands that make up the Estate outwith Threave Gardens. By making several detours, you can visit sections of the River Dee, the romantic castle and bird hides.

Distance:	6 miles/9.6km—this includes all the detours.
Time:	3 hours, maybe more, depending how long you stay at the castle and in the bird hides.
Map:	OS Landranger 84
Terrain:	Some sections can become muddy after wet weather or farm vehicle use.
NB:	The castle can be visited throughout the summer, from April 1 onwards. A fee is charged for visiting the island.

27

Ken-Dee Marshes Nature Reserve

Park in the Mains of Duchrae car park, grid ref. 695685, where there is an information board. The reserve lies on the west side of Loch Ken and the River Dee and is reached by a minor road off the B795 north of Glenlochar.

Ken-Dee Marshes. Look over the farmland near to the car park to see the main area for over-wintering geese, including a thousand or more greylag, 350 or so of the rare Greenland white-fronted geese and a smaller number of pink-footed and barnacle geese. In the woodland treecreepers, great spotted woodpeckers and willow tits reside throughout the year In summer they are joined by pied flycatchers, wood warblers and redstarts. Watch out, in autumn, for red squirrels coming down onto the side of the track to feed on

Walk 27

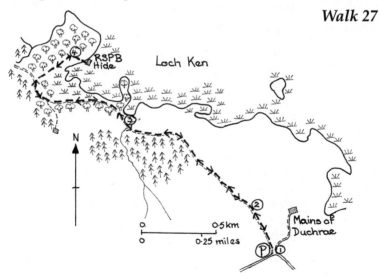

hazel nuts. The plants of the marshland provide dense cover for birds and from here you might hear, rather than see, grasshopper warblers and water rails. The hide at the end of your outward walk looks over marshland, open water, wet meadow and woodland.

1. Leave the parking area by a kissing gate. Here, in winter, you might spot a large flock of long tailed tits or a charm of goldfinches flitting excitedly through the surrounding bushes and trees. Pass the information board, where you can pick up a useful leaflet on the reserve. Continue along the delightful track, with open farmland to your right and conifers to your left.

2. Then the way is lined with mature beech where in winter redwing and fieldfare flock. Stroll on into mixed woodland, watching the trackside bushes as you go for the white flash of the rumps of a pair of colourful bullfinches and perhaps a diminutive goldcrest busily searching for insects in the lichen on the branches of hawthorn. Pause to read the explanatory plaques on the birds and plants you might spot.

3. And then the fences are gone and to the right the reed beds stretch towards the open water of Loch Ken. Carry on along the track and then turn right as directed by a white arrow. This pleasing footpath, after 450 yds, leads to the fine bird hide. Pause here to watch, in winter, for more fieldfares, teal, mallards, pintail and widgeon. In spring the bushes resound with the calls of migrants and throughout the year there is always a hungry sparrowhawk looking for a meal.

4. Return by the same route to the car park.

Practicals

Type of walk: A delightful short walk through deciduous woodland to a good bird hide which allows you to look over Loch Ken.

Distance: 3 miles/4.8km
Time: 1 ½ hours but build in time for watching the birds.
Map: OS Landranger 84.
Terrain: Level walk all the way. Footpath to hide can be muddy after rain.
NB: No dogs allowed.

28

The Glenkiln Sculptures

Park at the head of Glenkiln Reservoir, grid ref. 838785. It is reached by turning north off the A75, west of Dumfries, to the village of Shawhead. At Shawhead turn right and then almost immediately left.

In 1951, Sir William Keswick, the local landowner, began to collect a series of pieces by famous sculptors. He placed them, imaginatively, in various well chosen natural sites about the lonely small glen of Glenkiln.

John the Baptist by Auguste Rodin (1840–1917). This fine naked figure stands on a plinth at the head of the pretty Glenkiln reservoir.

Standing Figure by Henry Moore (1898–1986). An abstract sculpture placed near to Cornlee Bridge.

The King and Queen, by Henry Moore

Glenkiln Cross by Henry Moore stands high on the hill, on your right, as you walk beside the reservoir.

King and Queen by Henry Moore stands lower down the same hill. These two figures sit like an elderly couple, enjoying the tranquil stretch of water.

Visitation by Sir Jacob Epstein (1880–1959). This charming statue of the Virgin Mary stands among a group of pine trees.

Two Piece Reclining Figure No. 1 by Henry Moore. An abstract, enigmatic piece cast in fibreglass containing bronze dust.

Walk 28

1. From the parking area below the Rodin sculpture, pause to look out over the attractive reservoir, where you might see oyster catchers, lesser black backed gulls and greylag geese. Turn right and walk the minor road, with scattered deciduous trees and flowering gorse on the slopes to your right. Ahead is a plantation and through a gap in the trees you have a fine view of the northern hills. Just before the lane curves to cross Cornlee Bridge, look left to see Moore's Standing Figure.

2. Return along the lane and go on past the parking area. Look high on the hill, on your right, to see Moore's Glenkiln Cross. Continue on to a metal gate (the second on the right) immediately below Moore's King and Queen. Here, among the curlews, climb up the slope, cross a grassy track and go on a short distance to enjoy the charming, homely, piece. From here you might be tempted to wind your way up to the Cross.

3. Retrace your steps to the grassy track, crossed just above the metal gate, and head on along it as it rises gently to a gate. Beyond, stroll the continuing track through the rolling pastures, with pleasing

views of the reservoir below. Over the walls, to your left, you can spot the summit of Criffel. Carry on to come to the enclosure of Scots pines, among which stands the statue of the Virgin Mary.

Lapwing

4. Press on along the track to go through a gate to join a narrow road. Turn left and begin your steady descent through the remote countryside, where you might spot hares racing over the pastures. Look right as you go to see, on a small hillock, Moore's abstract piece. Enjoy the little burn, to your right, that hurries through its deep tree-lined ravine. Continue downhill to the T-junction.

5. Turn left. At the Y-junction keep left. As you pass through the deciduous trees on either side of the road, you might hear tawny owls calling and see red squirrels disporting. Stride on to come beside the reservoir to return to the parking area.

Practicals

Type of walk: A pleasing walk through a quiet pretty glen to visit six modern sculptures imaginatively set in lonely countryside.

Distance:	4 miles/6.5km
Time:	2–3 hours
Map:	OS Landranger 84
Terrain:	Easy walking all the way.

29

Manquhill

Park in the car park on the right side of the B729 just before Stroanpatrick Bridge, grid ref. 646918. This lies 7 ½ miles from Moniaive, where you leave the A702.

Southern Upland Way (SUW). This was officially opened in April 1984 and runs for 212 miles (340km) from Portpatrick on the south-western coast to Cockburnspath on the eastern seaboard. It passes through greatly varied country and from it the walker has some superb views. Much of the Way is hard-going and a challenge even to experienced walkers, but short stretches are suitable for families and less adventurous walkers. This walk and walks 3, 6, 12, and 15 in this book use parts of the Way.

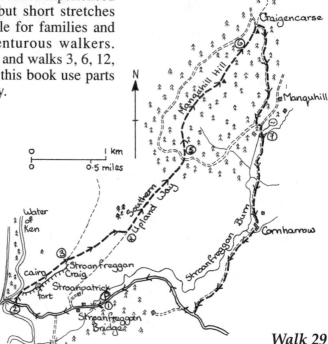

Walk 29

1. From the car park turn right (west) to cross Stroanpatrick Bridge. Continue on past Stroanpatrick farm, which lies back, right, from the road. Go on past a tin hut on the left and ignore the signposted SUW footpath on your right. This footpath will be joined later, enabling the walker to avoid a rather wet start.

2. A hundred yards before Smeaton's Bridge over the Water of Ken, turn right along a grassy reinforced track, with the river to your left. Climb the slope, enjoying the views, beyond the hurrying burn, of Cairnsmore of Carsphairn over the top of the huge conifer plantations. Continue on up, passing through the ramparts, gullies and fallen walls of an Iron Age fort. Admire the well chosen position, commanding the valley and the confluence of the Water of Ken and Stroanfreggan Burn. Go on to the cairn on the highest hillock of the ridge and pause to take in the rolling moorland. The austere landscape has very few traces of human habitation.

3. Carry on along the pleasing grassy ridge, well marked by tractor wheels, towards a small plantation. This lies to your left as the track descends to pass through a wall. Press on to see stone sheep pens ahead and, to their right, an ancient run-rig pasture enclosed by a ruinous wall. At this point you have joined the SUW.

4. Climb the stile and stroll on, with the wall to your right and SUW marker posts to your left. The way climbs steadily, wet in places, to a ladderstile at the junction of two walls. Beyond, the clear waymarked path, now well drained, goes on steadily uphill across the open hillside, passing through young conifers, allowing you a view of Cairnsmore of Cairsphairn, which has been lost to sight for a while. On reaching a forest road, cross and continue on the clearly marked path.

5. This narrow reinforced way, well cushioned by grass, takes you uphill and across a wide swathe of wet tussock grass between more young conifers. It is a pleasure to walk and as you go you can appreciate the effort that went into its construction. It leads onto the shoulder of Manquhill, Hill, with the indeterminate summit (1382 ft/421m) just to your right. At the brow of a steepish slope, with a marker post and another marker beside it, turn right and walk an indistinct path through the tussocky top to the ridge. Go on along the ridge, climbing small hillocks and then descending, only to climb again. Eventually after you have decided which is the highest point, and have enjoyed the glorious vista, return to the SUW, taking care

as you negotiate the ankle-twisting tussock grass, before walking on. Ahead you have an ever increasing view of Benbrack.

6. Carry on along the easy waymarked path, noting that a fox uses this route too. The Way keeps to the left of bun-shaped Craigencarse and then descends to a forest road in the col between Manquhill and Benbrack. Those wishing to climb Benbrack should continue on the SUW, but this walk leaves it here by turning right. Follow the forest road as it curves right and gently downhill, now below the slopes of Manquhill. Away to the left is a lonely cottage, once Manquhill farm. At the T-junction of tracks, turn left and, almost immediately, at the next T-junction, bear right, towards a bridge over the Stroanfreggan Burn. The gate here is locked but to its left is a stile, and a little scramble is required to return to the track.

7. Go on along the track over the open moor. After just over half a mile, you near the next dwelling, Cornharrow, with its pens of red deer. Here you might see wheatears, curlews, grey wagtails and oyster catchers about the walls and the burn. Keep to the right of the dwelling and, at the next locked gate, climb the stile beside it. Walk on along the low level forest track to join the B729, where you turn right. As you pass a small pond look for several pairs of teal. Go on along the almost traffic-free road to the parking area.

Wheatear

Practicals

Type of walk: A good circular hill walk through the lonely Southern Uplands.

Distance:	7 ½ miles/12.2km
Time:	3–4 hours
Map:	OS Landranger 77
Terrain:	Easy paths and tracks for most of the route. The first part of walk needs perseverance to find the tractor route. Not to be attempted in mist.

30

Scaur Water

Park in a large layby, just before the bridge over the Scaur Water, close to Arkland, grid ref. 805980. To reach this, leave the A702 by a narrow road, heading north, ½ a mile west of Penpont, signposted Knockelly. Remember not to obscure field gates or to park in signposted passing places.

Scaur Water. Take your time driving along the narrow road and walking along the west side of Scaur Water so that you may enjoy one of Nithsdale's loveliest glens.

Dippers. The dipper frequents rapidly moving streams. It is a rotund, short-tailed bird, dark above and white breasted. It is often

Scaur Water

Dipper

seen perching on rocks, around which the water swirls and tumbles, bobbing with spasmodic curtsies. When disturbed it flies rapidly and straight, with short whirring wings. From its rocky perch it will walk into the water and submerge, using its wings to progress after small creatures that forms its food. It nests by the water, often in a hollow between rocks or in a hole in the masonry of a bridge. Its song is a soft sweet whispering.

1. From the layby walk on along the lane to pass Arkland Cottage. Then cross the bridge over the Scaur, where you are likely to see grey wagtails and dippers in the pleasing burn below. Continue up the steepish hill, which is lined with bistort beneath hazel and thorn bushes. At the little triangle of roads, turn left. Press on along the high level narrow road, with rolling hills away to your left. The delightful lane continues past deciduous woodland where, below the trees in spring, flower bluebells, wild garlic, primroses and the delicate golden saxifrage. To your left flows the Scaur Water. Go over Woodend Burn, the haunt of more grey wagtails.

Walk 30

2. A quarter of a mile further along the road, (grid ref. 795997) take a reinforced track, on the right, crossing a pasture and leading into conifer woodland. A short steep climb

106

leads you out of the trees and then the track continues steadily upwards. Just before Woodend Cottage leave the track and walk a grassy trod, right, to a field gate in the wall ahead. Once through return up the slope, beyond the cottage, to rejoin the track, now a grassy way.

3. Walk on and then go through the gate in the wall on your left. Stroll the continuing grassy trod to enter a narrow plantation. Emerge from the trees and continue upwards. To your left you have a fine view of the huge cairn on Cairnkinna Hill and some walkers may wish to make a diversion, passing through the gate on your left, to climb to its summit (1815 ft/552m).

4. This walk continues along the clear way as it moves over to the side of the wall on the left, with a fine view down towards Druidhill Burn. Descend the track to pass to the right of barn before swinging right and going on down the glen beside a wall on the left. The gated track takes you through pleasing pastures and carries on to the left of dwellings at Merkland and then to a narrow road.

Oystercatcher

5. Walk on (right) along the pleasant way. Ignore the left turn at Druid Hall farm and stride on to pass the triangle of roads near to your parking place. Drop down to cross the bridge over Scaur Water, where you might spot the dippers and grey wagtails again.

Practicals

Type of walk: The walk starts along a delightful lane and continues easily over high moorland. The return is made along an equally pleasant lane.

Distance: 5 miles/8km
Time: 2–3 hours
Map: OS Landranger 78
Terrain: Some road walking. Clear paths over the moorland. The farm track may be muddy after rain.

31

Drumlanrig Castle and Country Park

Unlike Walk 32 this walk, though waymarked in parts, is not to be found in a trail leaflet.

To reach the castle take the A76 for three miles north from Thornhill. The access route is well signposted. To reach the car park, grid ref. 851994, drive up the access road to face the front of the castle The

Walk 31

parking area is on a sloping green to the right, opposite the 'Woodland Walks' mapboard, outside the castle stableyard.

Drumlanrig Castle. Nearly 700 years ago, Robert Bruce, King of Scotland, was ably supported by the Douglas family, notably Sir James, his right hand man. Their stronghold was at Drumlanrig—the hill (drum) at the end of a long (lang) ridge (rig). The present castle was built upon 15th century foundations by William Douglas, the 1st Duke of Queensberry, between 1679 and 1691. It was constructed from local sandstone at a time when architecture was in transition from fortified castles to peaceful palaces.

1. Stroll down the lime avenue, the approach road to the castle, and follow it as it swings right. Just before a causeway over a tributary stream, leave the road on the left, to walk over a small area of hillocks

and flats, a favourite place for a picnic. Pass through the small gate to the right of a farm gate. Beyond go on along a good path that hugs the edge of the slope that drops down to the wide, stately River Nith. The way passes through magnificent mixed woodland. Look for dippers on rocks in the river as you go. Dawdle this lovely stretch because all too soon the Nith almost disappears from sight as it flows through a sheer-sided tree-clad ravine.

2. Walk left as directed by a white arrow to join a pleasing track, along which you continue. From here you can glimpse the river but do take care if you decide to approach the precipitous edge. As you walk on you are accompanied by the sound of the Nith's cascades, waterfalls and rapids. A grassy way descends closer to the water's edge where you might spot a family of goosanders idling on the water. At any junction of tracks or paths always take the way nearest to the river until you emerge from the trees to see, below, several picturesque cottages.

River Nith at Drumlanrig

3. Here, in front of a gate to the first cottage, turn acute left to walk a reinforced track, which climbs steadily through woodland. The way then leaves the trees and goes on beside a thick beech hedge to your left and open pastures to your right. It then passes below a grand arch of more beech trees. Enjoy the fine views to the right of the Lowther hills and to the left of the Queensberry range—on a good day you can see Criffel and the hills of the Lake District.

4. At Sweetbit farm, turn right onto a metalled way and then left at a T-junction. Pass a white cottage on the right and walk on, enjoying the virtually traffic-free glorious high-level way. Pass a farm called Alton and beyond, where the road starts a series of sharp bends, turn right to stride a cart track.

5. At the cross of tracks, turn left and stroll on ahead. Where the fenced pasture ends on the left, turn left again to carry on along a wide grassy trod. (If this is still blocked with fallen larch, make a three-sided detour using forest rides, or climb the stile into the pasture and leave by another stile, opposite and slightly left.). Cross the forest road and go on along a fine grassy way. This is a glorious way where you might see roe deer and hear jays.

6. Where the pleasing track swings left towards a gate into pasture, press on ahead through the trees to a kissing gate onto a pasture, with a tall thin dwelling to your left. Go on to join the road taken at the start of the walk and turn right. Stride towards the castle, with the car park to your right.

Practicals

Type of walk: The grounds of the castle, the country park, are vast and walkers have open access. The woodlands, paths and tracks are a delight to walk. Footbridges take you easily across streams. After a severe gale some trees may have fallen but there is always a way around these blockages. It is also a working woodland and you should observe the diversion signs to avoid timber operations. There are no 'private' notices. A Countryside Ranger service operates on the estate to help and advise.

Distance: 7 miles/11.2km
Time: 3–4 hours
Map: OS Landranger 78

32

Drumlanrig Castle and Country Park

Walk 2 of the Park's Woodland Walks (Marr Burn)

Use the instructions for walk 31 to reach the castle and the parking area.

Woodland Walks. Three woodland walks have been excellently waymarked in the country park. Walk One, arrowed in orange and a mile in length, takes you to Beech Loch, a man-made pool constructed in the 19th century to enhance the picturesque layout of the park. The large beech trees overlooking the loch, which give their name to the pool, were planted as the pool was built. Walk two, Marr Burn (two miles and arrowed in red), is described below. Walk three, Mount Malloch, arrowed in yellow, is three miles long. It follows walks one and two to the bridge close to a waterfall and then follows a grassy path, which climbs gradually through woodland to the viewpoint and seat on the hill. Here you can enjoy the views of Upper Nithsdale and the Lowther Hills. A Countryside Ranger service operates on Drumlanrig Estate and the rangers are available to lead guided walks. You can also obtain helpful leaflets,

Bridge on Marr Burn, Drumlanrig

with maps and instructions, from their office. All three walks start close to the office, which is adjacent to the car park. Opposite the woodland walks mapboard, a finger post with all the coloured arrows upon it directs you uphill into the woods.

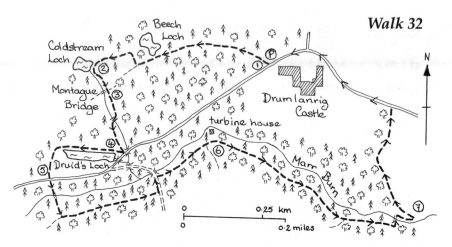

Walk 32

1. Take the grassy trod into the wood following the red waymarks. Pass through a kissing gate to walk a wide woodland path. At a Y-junction go on ahead to pass Beech Loch on your right, where there are picnic tables below the trees on the knoll. At the end of the small hillock, turn right and almost immediately left. Go on to pass Coldstream Loch, where broad-leaved pond weed, spearwort and water plantain thrive. The pretty loch, surrounded by fine mixed trees, is gradually silting up allowing willow scrub and reeds to encroach.

2. Turn left and follow the arrows directing you to Montague bridge. Pause to look at its fine construction. This bridge and others in the woods were built in the mid-nineteenth century. At this time 80 miles of driveway were laid out and small benches with stone uprights (many of which you pass or may sit on) were sited at good locations. All this work provided employment during a period of depression, besides improving the estate.

3. Take the descending steps to the left of the bridge and stroll the delightful path. Follow the waymarks right to cross the burn and go on downhill. Keep to the right of another fine bridge and descend to where there are more picnic tables.

4. Turn right to come to the Druid Loch. This pool may take its name from pagan acts of worship carried out here in ancient times. Today it provides a useful source of water in case of forest fires and here flourish water lilies and horse tails.

5. Continue on the path to cross the estate road and go on the waymarked route through hazel, larch and hawthorn. Cross the Marr Burn and carry on through the woodland. Turn left along a grassy ride and then bear left and then right along the burnside track, which passes a delectable waterfall. Ignore the next bridge on your left, and bear right to go on ahead (this is where the Mount Malloch yellow trail diverts from the red trail).

6. Look left to see the old turbine house, which once supplied the castle with electricity. Enjoy the continuing terrace above the burn, where you might see a mixed flock of tits sliding through the trees. Pass two seats before descending to the next waymark. Continue through a grassy glade to cross a footbridge over the Marr. Walk right to a stile into a pasture.

7. Turn left and follow the wall up to another stile under a lovely field maple. Continue ahead to reach an estate road, where you turn left to rejoin your car.

Red squirrel

Practicals

Type of walk: A pleasing stroll along good paths and tracks through deciduous woodland. To be enjoyed by all.

Distance:	2 miles/3.2km
Time:	1 ½ hours
Map:	Leaflet from Rangers Office or OS Landranger 78
Terrain:	Very easy walking.

33

Durisdeer, Roman Fortlet, Durisdeer Hill

Park by the church and the war memorial in Durisdeer, grid ref. 894037. To reach the small village, leave Carronbridge by the A702 and, after four miles, at Durisdeermill, take the signposted right turn.

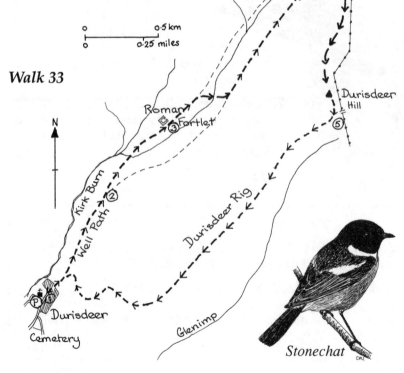

Walk 33

Stonechat

Durisdeer Church. The village, set among tall sycamore trees, is dominated by its surprisingly large church. It was built in 1699 by the first Duke of Queensberry of nearby Drumlanrig Castle (see walks 31 and 32). Look inside to see the magnificent Queensberry burial vault, and also the ancient box pews. By the front entrance to the church is a slab-topped tomb to the Covenanter Daniel MacMichael.

Roman Fortlet on the Roman Road. This fort would have been used by a detachment of 20 to 30 men to keep the remote stretch of road free from bandits. The road continued to Elvanfoot, where there was another Roman camp.

1. Stroll on along the road, with the church to your left, to a metal gate. Here a notice says that this is part of the Buccleuch Estate, which welcomes country lovers. Beyond the gate, stride the continuing rough track, known as the Well Path, an ancient route through the hills. This leads you along the glen, with the towering grassy slopes of Black Hill, and then Well Hill, to your left, and the heather clad slopes of Durisdeer Rig and Durisdeer Hill to the right. Walk on until you reach the signposted ladderstile over the wall on your left.

2. Climb the stile and follow the path to come to a small ford. Step across or, if it is in spate, move right to where the burn is narrower, and step across. Go on to climb the next stile and stroll on to the signpost beyond. This directs you sharp left to an easy approach to the square shaped fortlet, with its inner and outer ramparts. Pause here and enjoy the view over Nithsdale and the hills beyond—as the Roman guards did so many years ago. Listen for the curlews calling from the slopes.

3. Carry on along the clear track for a quarter of a mile, passing through a couple of gates. Then, look down right to spot a ladderstile over the wall, beyond the Kirk Burn, which hurries through the valley bottom. Drop down the slope, step across the burn and climb the stile. Walk ahead through clumps of low growing heather and then climb, quite steeply to the now delightful terraced path you left earlier. Look back across to the fortlet its good strategic position now seen to best advantage. Turn left and press on up the glen until you reach a gate on the saddle and the boundary of Dumfries.

115

4. Do not pass through but turn right and begin the steepish ascent beside the wall on your left. Occasionally it is better to move away from the boundary a little where the heather becomes ankle twisting. Watch for stonechats calling from the top of the heather shoots. Go on up and up until you reach the unmarked summit (1848 ft/ 569m). There is no cairn, just an extra tall fencepost from which the ground slopes gently away on all sides. Go on along the wall and continue beside it where it bends away left and comes close to a mound of eroded peat. Here a clear tractor-marked path continues beside the wall. Follow this easy-to-walk, airy way to a gate in the wall on your left. Do not go through.

5. Here follow the track as it swings right through the extensive heather moorland, where you might spot brown hares racing between the clumps of the sweet smelling plant. Stride on along the delightful way, with magnificent views in all directions. Soon you can spot the village huddled among its trees, with the tower of the church thrusting above them. Carry on the easy way as it bears towards the village and begins its zig-zagging descent, steeply at first and then more easily to come at last to the Well Path. Turn left and walk the few yards to the gate to the village.

Brown hare

Practicals

Type of path: A glorious walk into the lonely hills, with a visit to a Roman fortlet on the way

Distance: 4 ½ miles/7.1km
Time: 2–3 hours
Map: OS Landranger 78
Terrain: Track and path to Roman fortlet pleasant walking. Steep pathless climb beside the boundary wall. Excellent track for you gradual descent over Durisdeer Rig. Some steep grassy zig-zags to negotiate. A superb walk but not one to be attempted in mist.

34

The Forest of Ae

Park in the first reinforced bay, on the right, just inside the forest, grid ref. 980905. Leave Dumfries, north, by the A701. After 10 miles take the signposted left turn at Ae Bridge for Ae village. Continue past the houses for a further half mile to take, on your right, a forest road, marked by a large welcoming information board and a signpost denoting the start of a public footpath to Beattock. Follow the narrow road, cross the tractor bridge over the Windyhill Burn, and go on, bearing gently right, to reach the parking bay.

Rapids, Water of Ae

Ae village lies 336 ft/120m above sea level. It was built by the Forestry Commission to house workers and foresters. The name 'Ae', means 'water' in the old Scots. The name is recorded in the Guiness Book of Records as the shortest village name in Britain.

The Water of Ae, a dancing hurrying burn, passes north to south through the forest. Many small streams and tributaries feed into it and these add interest to the walk, making it sometimes a rather wet one.

Forest of Ae. The forest is situated among gentle rolling hills, which rise on the upper slopes of Queensberry Hill to more than 1650ft/500m above sea level. The forest has an open access policy but forestry operations may cause diversions. Please heed the warning signs. There are three waymarked routes in the forest: a riverside walk, Craigshiels walk and Greenhills walk. This walk makes use of parts of all three.

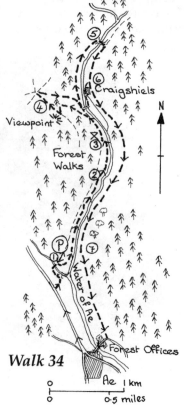

Walk 34

1. Walk back to the tractor bridge and, just before it, take a footpath going off left, and continuing beside the stream on your right. Gradually the stream moves away right and the path continues ahead into scrub. It then bears slightly right and then left and finally swings right again to come beside the Water of Ae. Go on along the waymarked (blue banded marker posts) path, walking upstream. The track occasionally brings you close to the forest road and sometimes along it for a few yards. Look out for a glade where early cultivation machines, brightly painted, are on display—these delight youngsters on this walk.

2. Go on to just past a small dammed pond and take the reinforced path off right that brings you close to the lovely stretch of water. Here in spring frogs and toads disport and

118

the water supports large patches of spawn. Here also you might spot herons enjoying the frogs! The path continues beneath Norway spruce, whose branches almost touch overhead, and then brings you to a large open picnic and parking area among cherry trees from where most forest walks start.

3. Join the road. Here you may wish to make a pleasing diversion for your picnic. If so, after 150 yards, take, on the left, the waymarked (red and blue bands) footpath into the forest. This climbs gently through the trees for more than a quarter of a mile before turning sharp left. It then climbs steepishly for a short distance to join a higher forest road. Opposite is Craigshiels viewpoint, with a picnic table just perfect for you to eat your sandwiches.

4. Walk on along the road; that is, on joining the road and ignoring the viewpoint, you turn right and stride the high level way to a junction of tracks. Turn sharp right to begin a delightful descent. Continue down between the mossy boulders edging the forest to pass through a gate. Beyond turn left onto the lower forest road and continue beside the Water of Ae. Ignore the first footbridge and stroll on, still with the burn to your right. It is edged with wood rush and scattered ash. Listen for goldcrests and coal tits in the trees to your left. Look for dippers atop rocks in the midst of the hurrying water. Perhaps you might also see a pair of goosanders.

Goosanders

5. Follow the road as it takes you across a bridge over the Ae where it descends in some dramatic cascades. To the right of the bridge is a deep brown pool, Dan's Pool, which takes many days in a good summer to be warm enough for most swimmers. Turn right to carry on along a fine forest road where you can look down on the surging river. On reaching Craigshiels—an old farm which is now being

renovated by the Scouts—you can choose to make an early return. If so, take the footpath on the right, just before the buildings. This returns you to the first bridge over the Ae. Once across, turn left to return along the forest road to the parking area.

6. The complete walk goes on along the pleasant forest road, with fine views of Queensberry Hill and of the valley below, its pastures soft green against a dramatic backcloth of larch and Norway spruce. Western hemlock, Douglas fir and Scots pine thrive here and are the haunt of siskin and crossbill. Listen as you go for emotive calls of tawny owls. Press on where the way climbs steadily and then pause and look back at the fine hills beyond the forest.

7. Soon the river and the forest road come close. Press on until you emerge from the trees to open pastures and a fine view across meadows to the village of Ae. Approaching the second cattle grid listen and look up to your left for the chatter of jays and the mewing of buzzards in this area of regenerating oak and hazel woodland. On reaching the metal road bear right to pass between the buildings of the Ae Forest Management complex. Cross the bridge over the Ae and walk on to the crossroads. Bear right along the road to take the signposted right turn into the forest. Cross the tributary burn and walk on to rejoin your car.

Practicals

Type of walk: A very satisfactory walk that takes you beside a delightful burn deep into a forest.

Distance:	Full route 7 miles/11.1km. Short cut across Craigshiels bridge, 5 miles/8km. Shortest route (no climb to Craigshiels viewpoint and taking the short cut) 4 miles/6.3km
Time:	3–4 hours, 2–3 hours, 1 ½–2 hours.
Map:	OS Landranger 78
Terrain:	Easy walking all the way. Take care when stepping over tree roots after rain. A short road walk, with little traffic.

35

Mabie Forest

Park in the car park, grid ref. 949712, at the start of the walk; a small parking fee has to be paid at an automatic kiosk on entry. The well signposted narrow road, leading into the forest, goes off west from the A710, five miles from Dumfries.

Mabie Forest. The Forestry Commission bought the forest in 1943. From about the year 1800, large numbers of trees were planted to enhance Mabie House. They were felled about a hundred years ago and many of the larger trees seen today are part of the first replanting.

This is a glorious walk, using parts of three of the Forestry Commission's trails. It is a grand forest for walkers, with good paths and tracks, well waymarked and with wonderful viewpoints and seats to enjoy them. The walk takes you through large areas of deciduous woodland and some conifers.

Mabie Forest provides for walkers, orienteers, cyclists, picnickers and those wishing to barbeque. It has an outdoor centre and an adventure playground. Its open access policy enables you to walk anywhere within its boundary.

Sulphur tuft and stag's horn fungus

Fungi. As you walk you might spot, at the right season, a plethora of fungi. They include: stinkhorns, which are difficult to spot in the undergrowth but which exude an unpleasant odour that is impossible to miss; honey fungus, on the base of birch trees; the diminutive bright orange-red stags horn (appropriately named); sulphur tuft, seen below conifers; and cup fungus, with its gills delicately turning up at the rim.

Walk 35

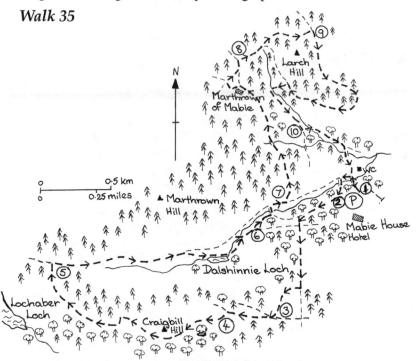

1. Descend to the bottom of the car park to come to several posts directing you on the various colour-banded walks. This walk first follows most of the brown banded posts and then some of the blue and finally the yellow Follow the winding track downhill to cross the Mabie Burn by a long, high footbridge. (For the toilets, strike right.) Turn left to walk beside the burn. In a few yards, turn left again to recross it and continue through some fine deciduous woodland. At the Y-junction bear right to follow the brown marker and go on ahead to cross a forest track.

2. Continue into conifers and go with the track as it winds right along the clear path. At the next banded marker, turn left to climb the slope to cross a wide track. Stroll on through western hemlock, climbing gently. The waymarkers are now conical-topped posts, painted bright red at the top. To the left, beyond a fence, is open pasture. Walk straight on, ignoring the first right turn. Continue to

where the way winds right. (Just before this right turn, and a few yards ahead, is a seat where you can pause to enjoy a first view of the Nith valley.)

3. Stride on to come to a forest road, turn right and then leave it almost immediately, left. Stroll uphill through a clear felled area already well colonised by burgeoning vegetation, including the attractive hard fern. Go on up some railed steps, following the brown banded posts. Continue on the narrow path, along the edge of conifers and then into a lovely corner of scattered oaks.

4. The path leads into a clearing, where there is a seat constructed around the huge trunk of a massive ancient sycamore. Climb the railed steps to come suddenly upon a spectacular view of Criffel and the Waterloo Monument above New Abbey. Go on to a granite knoll to spot where the River Nith enters the Solway. Pass several seats and then follow the path as it descends gently, with Lochaber Loch and its anglers far below to the left.

5. At the forest road turn right. Ignore the next right turn and then go on ahead, avoiding a branch of the road which swings left. Further on a narrow path leads downhill, right, towards a small pool, and then comes beside the delightful Dalshinnie Loch. At the far end, by the dam, is a seat. Beyond, the waymarked trail continues, gradually bearing left to join a glorious widish path through deciduous woodland, where you walk right to continue. If this way is blocked by forestry operations, return to the forest road and turn right.

6. Watch out for the railed waymarked left turn that eventually brings you to railed steps to go over Mabie Burn. Walk on to join the forest road and bear right to a wide cross of tracks. Here you may wish to go on ahead and then right to the car park.

7. This walk bears left for a steepish climb up the access road to the outdoor centre, the posts now marked with blue bands. At the centre, bear left behind the white cottage and then, very shortly at a Y-junction, right onto a knoll, which has picnic tables with a pleasing view of the Nith and the Solway. Leave the knoll by grassy steps to return to the road and continue on (left) to the next Y-junction.

8. Bear right and walk on to take the next left turn. This diversion is not on a trail but the wide grassy track, initially wet, soon becomes easy to walk. At the col just before the track climbs steeply, turn left to descend a narrow path to a forest track and yellow banded posts.

123

9. Turn right to begin a fine high level walk overlooking the river valley. There are several seats situated just off the track on the left where you can enjoy the charming pastoral view. Follow the track as it winds round right and look for the railed waymarked stepped way, descending through trees, on the left. At its foot go on left to follow the blue and yellow banded posts.

10. Take the waymarked left turn leading to railed steps to cross a burn and go on. By a raised wooden way, on the right, bear right after it and follow the path to come to the cleared area, where the toilets lie to your left. Continue on to cross the sturdy high level footbridge crossed earlier and follow the track to return to the car park.

Green woodpecker

Practicals

Type of walk: Easy walking on good paths and tracks, with several magnificent viewpoints.

Distance:	6 ½ miles/10.5km. You may have to add another mile if you have to make detours because of fallen trees, caused by windblow, blocking the trails.
Time:	3 hours
Map:	Use the excellent leaflet 'Forests of Solway, Forest Walks' or OS Landranger 84
Terrain:	Some tracks cross clear felled areas and these need care when stepping over fallen twigs, especially after rain.

Sweetheart Abbey and the Waterloo Monument

There is a well signposted large parking area, with toilets, beside Sweetheart Abbey, grid ref. 964664, in the village of New Abbey. To reach the village take the A710 for six miles, south from Dumfries.

Sweetheart Abbey. The monks named their abbey, Sweetheart as a tribute to their founder, Lady Devorgilla de Balliol, the devoted wife of John Balliol. He died in 1269 and Devorgilla always carried with her his embalmed heart in a beautiful casket. In 1273 she signed a charter to found the new abbey in memory of her husband. She and the casket were buried in the abbey in 1289, when she died, aged 80. The abbey, in the pretty village of New Abbey, lies between the granite bulk of Criffel and the wide-flowing Nith estuary. The glorious red sandstone ruin, a delight to visit, is enclosed by a granite wall, built with stone hewn from the granite boulders cleared from the site; the sandstone came from across the Nith. The village is so named because Sweetheart Abbey was the youngest of three Cistercian abbeys established in Galloway.

Waterloo Monument. The 65 ft high tower stands on an open eminence, in the conifer forest, overlooking New Abbey. It was completed in 1816 as a tribute to the valour of British, Belgian and Prussian soldiers who, under Wellington and Blucher, defeated the French at the battle of Waterloo—18 June 1815. It has a spiral staircase which leads to the open unprotected top. There is no parapet and care should be taken when enjoying the view, particularly if accompanied by children.

New Abbey Cornmill. This stands at the opposite end of the village to the abbey. The present building dates from the 18th

Waterloo Monument, New Abbey

century and is believed to have replaced an earlier cornmill worked for and by the monks.

1. Turn right out of the car park and walk through the village. Go past the Abbey Arms and bear left. Turn left at the signpost for the pedestrian way to the Waterloo Monument, to walk beside the attractive mill pond and its leat. Go on along a tarmacked lane, walled on either side. Follow it as it rises steadily and swings left, with views down to the village and the abbey. Go on as the lane veers right, with a pleasing view of the monument on the right and of Criffel ahead.

2. At the end of the metalled way, walk ahead ignoring, on the right, the track to a white building and, on the left, a wooden bridge over Glen Burn. Climb the stile and go on along a raised way beside the stream on your left. Follow the path as it quickly swings right, beyond a small pasture, and then climbs several granite steps to cross a track. Walk on for a few more paces and then begin the long, steep, stepped climb that takes you up through conifers.

3. Pause regularly to look back down through the trees to see the River Nith on its way to join the Solway and for a grand view of Criffel. Continue on up the granite stairway to pass out of the trees to enjoy more spectacular views. A few more steps and the dramatic tower lies ahead, from where you can see Dumfries across a vast stretch of pleasing countryside.

4. After your descent from the tower, continue on the clear path, signposted 'easier path'. Descend down a conifer-needle strewn

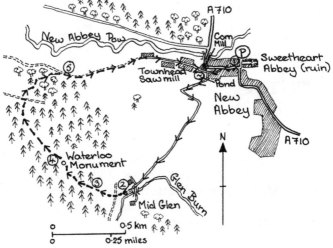

path to a waymark, with an arrow and a little white tower on it, to turn left and then wind right as directed by another waymark. Stroll on the glorious way to come to a lively burn, where another waymark sends you right. This delightful way passes through ancient deciduous woodland where many small birds flit through the branches and the lush undergrowth.

5. Join a cart track and turn right. Soon the track becomes metalled and goes past a large timber yard. It then passes the other side of the mill pond. To visit the mill, which is well worth the effort, turn left.

Practicals

Type of walk: The steep slope up to the monument, by granite steps, makes for a challenging climb. The return through mixed woodland is most enjoyable.

Distance:	2 ½ miles/4km
Time:	2 hours
Map:	OS Landranger 84
Terrain:	Paths can be muddy after rain.

37

Criffel

There is limited parking by Ardwall farm, grid ref. 970635. To reach this parking area, drive south along the A710 from New Abbey. After two miles turn right into the narrow access lane to the farm. Here you are asked to park on the right verge so that you do not obstruct the farm traffic.

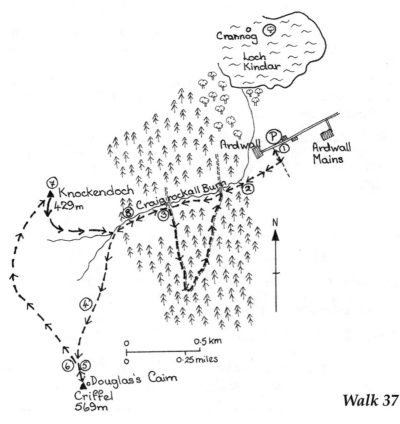

Walk 37

Criffel (1868ft/569m) is a small mountain. Its name is believed to mean raven's hill and over it ravens do soar and utter their raucous calls. It rises abruptly from the shores of the Nith estuary and its homely outline can be seen from so many directions that it seems like an old friend once you come to climb it. At 1868 ft it is a modest climb but one that should not be underestimated. Do not attempt in mist when the summit can be misleading—and what's the point when you can't enjoy the magnificent views from the summit?

Criffel from Caerlaverock

1. From the parking area, go through a large gate on the left as directed by a signpost, which says 'Criffel walk 2 miles'. Take the first right and pass through the right of two gates to walk a grassy walled track. Go through another gate into the forest.

2. Walk straight ahead following the waymark along a pleasing path, soon to come close to the tumbling Craigrockall Burn on your right. Cross the forest road and go on, continuing through the forest beside the noisy cascading burn. The peaty way is clear to follow but after rain can be muddy and some boulder hopping is required as well as scrambling round and over the granite boulders, which give a good grip to your boots.

3. Cross another forest road and go on the waymarked path which can, in parts, be quite boggy, to come to a stile over the forest fence. Ahead is a fine view of the steep path towards the summit. To the right stands Knockendoch (1476 ft), a shapely subsidiary summit. Bear slightly left to cross more bog and then climb steeply through great banks of heather, choosing the driest way. At the heather line, the path goes on steeply upwards, much drier underfoot for a short distance. Pause here to enjoy the marvellous view across

129

the Nith estuary to the Caerlaverock nature reserve. Look also for New Abbey village and its abbey, with Dumfries in the distance. You can also see much of Loch Kinder, glimpsed from the car park—its 'crannog', a man-made island once approached by a causeway, is to the left of a larger island.

Peregrine falcon

4. The clear way continues, wetter again, but there is always a way around the boggy patches. Towards the summit you bear left after joining a path that comes in on your right—the way you go to Knockendoch.

5. Go on to the granite plateau of the summit. You reach, first, a large cairn of stones with a stick projecting, flagpole-like, out of its top. It is known as Douglas's Cairn. A few yards beyond is the trig point, with a simple boulder shelter around it. The views are tremendous. You can see much of the Solway, the Lake District hills and the Southern Uplands. Return to the cairn and walk along the approach path.

6. Ignore the steep slope ascended earlier and walk ahead in the direction of Knockendoch. A clear path descends to the col, again wet in places. It bears slightly left to avoid the wetness and then continues on unswervingly to the fine summit, with more extensive views.

Raven

7. Ignore the good track dropping off the plateau in the direction of New Abbey—that way will involve a two-mile walk back along the A710 to your car. Instead descend slightly south of east. There is no path and the way is through tiresome heather. Descend over what grassy areas there are (green grass, not orange-tipped—the latter is purple moor grass and grows in ankle wrenching tussocks) and follow intermittent grassy trods used by deer.

Soon you can spot, below, the stile taken earlier into the forest. A narrow path takes you d o w n h i l l towards it.

Oystercatchers

8. Beyond the stile, continue along the path to the forest road. Here turn right and stride the easy way, a great relief after your steep descent. Follow the road as it winds round left and comes to the short path, right, to the gate to the grassy track. At the end of this, turn left and pass through the large gate to rejoin your car.

Practicals

Type of walk: An exhilarating, challenging walk followed by a pathless descent into the forest from Criffel's subsidiary. Suitable for fell walkers.

Distance:	4 ½ miles/7.1km
Time:	3–4 hours
Map:	OS Landranger 84
Terrain:	Walking boots are essential to negotiate the wet areas, the boulders and the banks of heather. The forest road is a pleasant relief.

38

Caerlaverock Castle and National Nature Reserve

In winter it is possible to park in the castle car park, grid ref. 026657. The fee charged entitles you to visit the castle. On a busy summer day there may not be space so walkers are asked to park half a mile south-west along the road (see map).

Caerlaverock Castle. The warm pink sandstone walls and jagged towers reflected in the glass-like waters of the moat make it every visitor's idea of a fairytale castle. It was built securely on rock by the Maxwell family in the 1270s. It replaced an earlier one built, in the 1220s, too close to the salt marshes of the Solway—these have since receded. Sieges and battles, resulting in damage to the castle, continued throughout the centuries but with the accession of James VI of Scotland to the English throne in 1603, peace came to the border country. In 1634 Robert Maxwell, Earl

Caerlaverock Castle

Nithsdale, began to build a new house within the castle and today you can still see the wonderful allegorical carvings over the windows built into the structure. But in 1640, after a siege during the Civil War, the Royalist garrison surrendered to the Covenanters and the castle was partially dismantled.

Barnacle Geese. If you visit the nature reserve in late September or early October you will be astounded by the huge skeins of geese coming in over Criffel's long ridge. On a day with a strong north-westerly blowing, they arrive in their hundreds to join the thousands already grazing on the pastures close to the shore. Here they rest after their migratory flight from Spitzbergen, within the Arctic Circle. Watch out for a peregrine putting them up in their thousands. Then they wheel and dive,

Barnacle geese

forming black clouds, and gabbling like excited puppies as they go.

1. Return along the access road of the castle or walk the road (¼ mile) from the marsh car park to this point. (See end of walk for an alternative route from the marsh car park.) Pause on the edge of the B-road to view the walled copse on the summit of Ward Law, the site of an Iron Age fort. To reach it, cross the road and walk ahead along a hedged and fenced track to go through a gate. Walk up beside the hedge on your left, where you might spot the pretty heartsease growing among a root crop. Go through the next gate and turn right to continue beside a fence on your right. As you near the hill recross the fence by a stile and then climb the ladderstile onto the mound. Wander at will over the well placed site and pause to enjoy the wonderful views.

2. Return to the B-road and turn left to walk for half-a-mile. Pass through the few cottages at Shearington and then take a narrow metalled road on the right to walk for a mile over the flat pastures in the direction of the Wildfowl and Wetlands Trust (WWT) at Eastpark Farm.

Walk 38

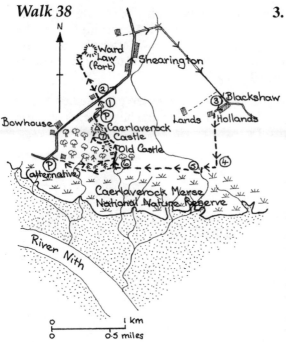

3. At the cottages at Blackshaw turn right, in the opposite direction to the WWT farm access road. Enjoy the fine view over to Ward Law, the only high ground to be seen (except for Criffel), and walk on to a house named Hollands. It has a fine barn with external steps. Here the road walking is over. Just before the dwelling, go through a gate into a delightful grassy track.

4. Stroll to a stile to the nature reserve. Here a vast area of great reed stretches away to the shore and the cacophony of the geese can be heard. Turn right as directed by the arrow and walk a grassy path that leads out onto the Merse March (see map). At the fence bear left. Cross duckboards and a footbridge onto a floodbank, where you turn right for your mile long walk over the marsh.

5. Pause here to see Ward Law again and then walk the path. As you go listen for curlews calling from the shore and watch for snipe as they are disturbed from probing the mud. Soon the way becomes less easy to walk and here walking poles will help you step from one tussock of the floodbank to the next—between the tussocks are pockets of mud best avoided. Eventually the path improves as you near the corner of a wood ahead. On firmer ground look for stonechats on top of the gorse bushes and meadow pipits and skylarks flitting among the tussocks. Here you might be fortunate to see a huge flock of oyster catchers put up by a 'teasing' peregrine.

6. Cross a ladderbridge over an inlet and continue to a stile. Bear right into the forest and, ignoring the left turn, walk ahead through

134

the delightful mixed woodland, which provides a marvellous contrast after your crossing of the Merse. Join a track to pass in front of several cottages to come to the mound of the old castle. Here use the viewing platforms to see the foundations revealed during an archaeological dig.

7. Just beyond turn left and follow a delightful path through woodland. The way, over intermittent duckboarding, leads you out of trees to come, suddenly, upon a magical view of the castle.

NB If you have had to park at the marsh car park, take the path at the end of the parking area. Walk ahead with the marsh on your right. At a Y-junction take the left branch into delightful woodland. The path joins the walk just after point 6 (it is the left turn mentioned) and from there continue to the castle (and your visit to it) and then carry on with the rest of the walk. On returning from the circular ramble, do not take the stile into the wood but continue along the marsh following the waymarks to join the path back to the car park. This alternative avoids your either missing out the castle or retracing part of your route.

Practicals

Type of walk: Nearly two miles of walking along minor roads. The way along the Merse (marsh) can be very wet and needs care; best attempted when the tide is low.

Distance: 5 miles/8km
Time: 3 hours plus bird-watching time
Map: OS Landranger 84

39

The Devil's Beef Tub

Park outside the Annan Water Hall, grid ref. 076104, a small community centre with limited parking space. You are asked not to obstruct the gates to pastures. To reach the centre from Moffat, take the A701 north, but leave the main road on the outskirts of the town, where it bears left by a church, and take the minor road that continues ahead (slightly right). Follow this road for three miles. If the parking space is full, seek a convenient verge.

The Devil's Beef Tub. This huge natural depression is found among wild hills, five miles north-west of Moffat. It gained its name from having been used by Border 'reivers' in the 18th century to hide stolen cattle. These animals were black Galloways, which then formed the basis of the region's economy. Annanhead Hill (1323 ft/478m) lies to the north of the tub, looking down on the source of the River Annan.

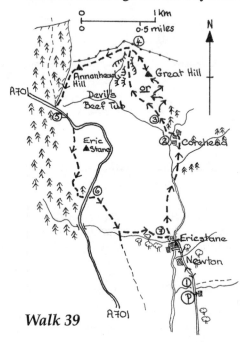

Moffat. An elegant town, was once a well known Scottish spa where it is said James Boswell, friend of Dr Johnson, was restored to health. The former pump room and baths now house the town hall. It is a well kept town, with plenty of pleasant shops, hotels, and flower gardens.

Walk 39

1. Stroll on along the valley road, with a fine view of the hills to your right. Ignore the right of way to Hart Fell spa. Continue past a dwelling named Newton. Bear left and then quickly right at the farm of Ericstane, where a small burn flows to your left. Cross the footbridge and walk on, slightly right between farm buildings, and then bear right again (ignoring the gated track—your return route) to walk the delightful track. Cross the burn again by a wide plank bridge and walk on through the quiet glen, heading towards a farm. Cross the stream again. Ignore the house to your left to pass between a white cottage and its outbuildings.

2. Go ahead. Step across the burn and take a gate on the left of a small plantation which supports an extensive rookery. Wind right, round the wood, ignoring the continuing grassy terraced way, and go on beside the trees. Go through the gap in the fence ahead and then strike away from the trees, across the pasture, to a tied wooden gate in the fence to your left.

3. Here a decision has to be made. The continuing path ascends steadily and pleasingly at first but, after eventually winding round the shoulder of the hill and into the cleft between Annanhead Hill and Great Hill, it becomes 'white knuckle', with sheer steep drops into the 'Tub'. It is a good path but one that should be tackled only by sure-footed walkers with a head for heights. A safer way is to climb the end of Great Hill, zig-zagging up the pathless steepish way, keeping slightly to the west, (left) of Skirtle Craig, to the cairnless summit (1320 ft/466m). From here head on west, following tractor marks (boundary fence to your right) to come to the col, the head of the ravine—which you would have reached if you had taken the narrow path. Here you might disturb a merlin.

4. By whichever route you have reached this point, continue on beside the boundary fence and then follow a good grassy trod across the sward. As it ascends it steadily moves away from the fence to arrive at the summit cairn of Annanhead Hill. Pause here to enjoy the superb views and then continue on the clear path in the direction of the A701. Climb a broken stile and continue beside the fence. Carry on to a sliding gate to the side of the A-road.

5. Turn left and walk the verge, with care. Cross to take a tied gate on the opposite side of the road. Beyond walk the faint path and go on where it becomes much clearer. At a Y-junction, follow the tractor marks, left, to continue behind Ericstane Hill. The track goes on

downhill to pass through a gate into a mixed planting of young trees. Carry on the track as it continues downhill to the road. Cross with care to walk on down a good track.

Merlin

6. As you stride the grassy way listen for skylarks, meadow pipits, lapwings and curlews. After just under half a mile, turn left through a farm gate. Press on for nearly half a mile down the wide, sometimes muddy track, in the direction of Ericstane farm, passed at the outset of the walk. As you descend enjoy the marvellous view ahead. Before the gate in the valley bottom, look right to see if you can discern the double ramparts of an ancient fort.

7. Turn right beyond the gate to return along the lane to where you have parked.

Practicals

Type of walk: This walk takes you round a dramatic natural depression. It starts along a good track and then ascends by a faint path, or pathless, over or around Great Hill to continue onto Annanhead Hill. The return is made along clear tracks

Distance: 6 miles/9.6km
Time: 3–4 hours
Map: OS Landranger 78
Terrain: Make a wise choice for how you climb Great Hill. Children and dogs should be under firm control.

40

The forts and settlements of Castle O'er forest

Park in the Bessie's Hill parking area, in Castle O'er forest, grid ref. 250953. To reach this, drive to the south end of Eskdalemuir village. Beyond, where the B709 bends sharply left, go ahead along a minor road, keeping the White Esk to your left and then, after pastures, the forest on your right, until you reach the car park.

Bessie's Hill settlement. Celtic tribes of the Iron Age built their settlements in prominent places. Bessie's Hill settlement, probably inhabited by people of the Selgovae tribe, commanded a sweeping vista of the Eskdale valley below. From the site the occupants could see and be seen. The settlement was surrounded by ramparts and ditches, which you can still see today.

Bessie's Hill fort. On a spur of land below the settlement stands the fort. It had high ramparts and deep ditches, the outlines of which can still be traced. A Forest Enterprise information panel says the warriors of a Celtic tribe were protectors and champions, important

Bessie's Hill fort, O'er forest

people within society. Celtic warfare was not about armies of invaders but about cattle raids and single combat between chariot driving champions. Cattle and the decapitated heads of their enemies were the prizes of such fights.

Castle O'er Hill Fort. The community that lived in this larger hill fort was probably a very important branch of the Selgovae tribe. The fort would have been surrounded by earthworks, banks and ditches, dividing the rich open grasslands of the valley into fields and corrals for the livestock of the community.

NB. At the time of writing much of the extensive forest had been clear-felled and acres of tree stumps and tangled brashings gave the forest a dreary air. However, the spectacular hill forts set the imagination afire and amply made up for the forest roads.

1. Take the waymarked footpath on the right at the entrance to the car park. Follow it through the trees to the top of a flight of wooden steps. Cross the forest road and head straight uphill to the Iron Age settlement. Return to the road and turn right. A few yards along bear left and then right through the trees to come to Bessie's Hill fort. Wander around the double ramparts and along the ditches of

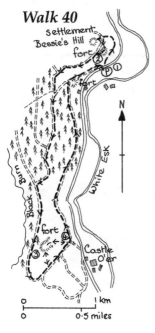

Walk 40

this strategic site, from where you can look down steeply, through the trees, in the direction of the car park.

2. Return to the forest road and turn left to walk on. At the Y-junction take the waymarked left branch. At the T-junction, turn right and go on to pass a pond with a small island. From here you have a good view of the pretty valley of the White Esk. And then the trees close in on either side. Follow the forest road as it winds right. At the T-junction turn left, continuing past a hillock of Scots pine. Look down right to see the meanders of Black Burn.

3. Follow the road as it winds left, climbing steadily. Where a forest road comes in on the right, climb left along two parallel rough ditches. These are

earthworks of Castle O'er Iron Age hill fort, where cattle would have been coralled. At the wire fence follow the waymarks directing you right along it to an entrance to this dramatic site. Once within the fort look for traces of roundhouses; each of these would have accommodated an extended family safe within the mighty ramparts and ditches. The hilltop was probably inhabited for more than 500 years until it was abandoned some time after the Roman occupation. You will wish to linger here and let your imagination have free play before you return to the road.

4. Ignore the right turn and continue on the high level way, with a fine view over the White Esk. At the T-junction look right to see the less dramatic traces of Castle Hill fort. Follow the track as it winds right and leads down to the car park.

Buzzards

Practicals

Type of walk: A satisfactory walk within an extensive forest to visit several intriguing Celtic sites.

Distance: 4 ½ miles/7.2km
Time: 2–3 hours
Map: OS Landranger 79
Terrain: All the forest roads are well graded and pleasant to walk.

Clan Walks

A series of walks described by Mary Welsh, covering some of the most popular holiday areas in the Scottish Highlands and Islands.

Titles published so far include:

1. 44 WALKS ON THE ISLE OF ARRAN
2. WALKS ON THE ISLE OF SKYE
3. WALKS IN WESTER ROSS
4. WALKS IN PERTHSHIRE
5. WALKS IN THE WESTERN ISLES
6. WALKS IN ORKNEY
7. WALKS ON SHETLAND
8. WALKS ON ISLAY
9. WALKS ON CANNA, RUM, EIGG & MULL
10. WALKS ON TIREE, COLL, COLONSAY AND A TASTE OF MULL
11. WALKS IN DUMFRIES AND GALLOWAY

OTHER TITLES IN PREPARATION

Books in this series can be ordered through booksellers anywhere. In the event of difficulty write to Clan Books, The Cross, DOUNE, FK16 6BE, Scotland.